WHAT DO WE *KNOW* ABOUT
THE AMERICAN REVOLUTION?

"The British are coming!" shouted Paul Revere.

"If they mean to have a war, let it begin here!" said Captain John Parker on Lexington Green in the predawn light of April 19, 1775.

"Don't fire till you see the whites of their eyes!" yelled Colonel Prescott at Bunker Hill.

When asked about the American Revolution, many Americans remember only a few "historic" quotations like these. But each quotation is questionable because (1) no authenticated contemporary accounts verify that these words were spoken by these men, and (2) given the historical context, it is unlikely that these people would have expressed their thoughts in precisely these words.

For example, Paul Revere would have said "the Regulars" were coming, not "the British," since all colonists considered themselves British Americans before war broke out and sides were taken.

IS IT MYTH OR REALITY?

Here are more myths that are often accepted as authentic fact:

Myth: Most of the early action of the war took place in Boston.

Reality: As described in this book, other towns, from Cambridge to Concord, were involved in the start of the Revolution, as were other colonies.

Myth: All American colonists supported the Revolutionary War effort.

Reality: Only about one third of Americans were patriots, one third were Tories loyal to the king, and the other third were neutral or indifferent.

Myth: Colonial patriots consisted exclusively of white Protestant males of British descent.

Reality: American patriots included in their ranks many diverse people (see this book's chapters on women, children, blacks, Jews, and Native Americans).

Myth: The American Revolution was less significant than other wars, such as the Civil War.

Reality: Colonial patriots risked their lives to guarantee rights that, after independence, became guaranteed in the U.S. Constitution and its Bill of Rights. Their actions laid the foundation for America's greatness and inspired other freedom-fighters around the world.

Myth: We have nothing new to learn about the American Revolution today.

Reality: As this book explains, historians continue to study and reinterpret this important chapter in our history.

For every visitor to eastern Massachusetts, a wealth of discoveries await— in the pages of this guide and among the cities and towns, houses and greens, monuments and churches, and other sites waiting to be explored in . . .

REVOLUTIONARY BOSTON, LEXINGTON AND CONCORD

A few weeks after the battles of Lexington and Concord, Connecticut militiamen Ralph Earle and Amos Doolittle visited the battle sites and interviewed people who had witnessed the events of April 19, 1775. The four drawings created by Earle and engraved by Doolittle are the closest we will ever come to witnessing these historic events. Doolittle did not credit Earle for many years (perhaps because Earle became a Tory), and the four images are now commonly referred to as the Doolittle Prints. Shown here is "The Engagement at the North Bridge in Concord." At the beginning of Part I is "The Battle of Lexington." Part II opens with "A View of the South Part of Lexington," showing fighting along the Battle Road. Part III opens with "A View of the Town of Concord," which shows British Regulars marching into the center of Concord. (Connecticut Historical Society)

Revolutionary Boston, Lexington and Concord

★ ★ ★ ★ ★ ★ ★ ★ ★ ★ ★ ★ ★ ★ ★ ★ ★ ★ ★

The Shots Heard 'Round the World!

Third Edition
Joseph L. Andrews, Jr., MD
and Contributors

Commonwealth Editions
Beverly, Massachusetts

"The Freedom Trail" is a registered trademark of the Freedom Trail Foundation, permission of which is gratefully acknowledged.

Cover photos: *The Battle of Lexington,* anonymous, evidently based on Amos Doolittle's 1775 print (Corbis); Paul Revere statue (Susan VanEtten); reenactors on Concord's North Bridge (National Park Service, Minute Man National Historical Park).

ISBN-13: 978-1-889833-22-4
ISBN-10: 1-889833-22-3

Library of Congress Cataloging-in-Publication Data

Andrews, Joseph L. (Joseph Lyon), 1938–
    Revolutionary Boston, Lexington, and Concord : the shots heard 'round the world / Joseph L. Andrews, Jr. and contributors.--3rd ed.
        p. cm.
        Rev. ed. of: Revolutionary Lexington & Concord. 1st ed. 1998.
        Includes bibliographical references and index.
        ISBN 1-889833-22-3 (pbk. : alk. paper)
        1. Concord, Battle of, 1775. 2. Lexington, Battle of, 1775. 3. Battlefields--Massachusetts--Concord--Guidebooks. 4. Battlefields--Massachusetts--Lexington (Town)--Guidebooks. 5. Concord (Mass.)--Guidebooks. 6. Lexington (Mass. : Town)--Guidebooks. 7. Minute Man National Historical Park (Mass.)--Guidebooks. I. Andrews, Joseph L. (Joseph Lyon), 1938– Revolutionary Lexington & Concord. II. Title

    E241.C7 A54 2002
    973.3'311—dc21

                                                                2001055530

Publication history
Concord Guides Press: First edition, April 1998; second edition, April 1999
Commonwealth Editions: Third edition, February 2002 (third printing, August 2005)

Cover and text design: Jill Feron/Feron Design
Photo research: Susan Van Etten
Index: Dan Connolly

Commonwealth Editions is an imprint of Memoirs Unlimited, Inc.
266 Cabot Street, Beverly, Massachusetts 01915
www.commonwealtheditions.com

Visit the author on the Web at www.concordguides.com and www.concordpress.com.

Contents

★ ★ ★ ★ ★ ★ ★ ★ ★ ★ ★ ★ ★ ★ ★

Statue of the Concord Minute Man by Daniel Chester French, 1875.
(Susan VanEtten)

Preface to the Third Edition
with Acknowledgments

★ ★ ★ ★ ★ ★ ★ ★ ★ ★ ★ ★ ★ ★ ★

When I moved to Concord in 1995, I learned as much as I could about Concord's extraordinary colonial, Revolutionary, literary, and natural heritage. I discovered that I had a great interest in these topics, perhaps partly because I am descended from at least three men who participated in the Revolutionary War. After passing an extensive exam, I became a Licensed Concord Guide. I volunteered at the Concord visitor information booth. And, after starting Concord Guides Walking Tours with others, I personally guided visitors from around the world through this rich and varied national treasure.

I was frequently asked if there was a good introductory guidebook to the history of the area, one that was accurate, readable, succinct, and affordable. There were volumes at both ends of the spectrum—from slim brochures to weighty academic tomes—but I knew of nothing in the middle, no comprehensive guidebook with the features visitors seemed to desire.

With the sort of optimism and chutzpah that only a naïve newcomer can muster I decided to combine my experience as a freelance writer with my curiosity about history and write the book myself. After several publishers rejected my proposal, I decided to publish the book myself. Suffice it to say, I made many mistakes. But with the help of Jim Steinmann of Minute Man Press in West Concord, who met my unreasonable requests with hard work and a smile, we printed the book by my self-imposed deadline of Patriots' Day 1998, with only hours to spare. Reactions to the first edition were generally positive, and we sold out in several months.

A few critics complained about what our short (sixty-four-page) book did *not* have. Why all the material on Lexington and Concord's roles in the Revolution? How about more details on Boston? And how about Arlington, Acton, Cambridge, and other towns along or near the Battle Road? Hence, the second edition of April 1999—which included not only chapters on Boston and other towns but also sections on the Revolutionary contributions of often overlooked groups, namely women, blacks, and Native Americans. We also added more photos and tables. This new edition was well received and sold more widely than the first.

To produce the present third edition, I happily teamed up with Commonwealth Editions; its publisher, Webster Bull; and his staff. The entire narrative has been reedited and expanded to include chapters on events leading up to the American Revolution and Boston's Freedom Trail. To better portray the diversity of the Revolutionary effort, we also added chapters on the roles of children and Jews. And many new illustrations have been added, including both present-day photographs of historic sites and period illustrations demonstrating how each era has viewed the events of the Revolution through its own subjective lens.

★ ★ ★

My deepest thanks go to Webster Bull for his foresight in agreeing to publish this third edition and to give it wider distribution. My gratitude also extends to the staff of Commonwealth Editions—to Susanna Brougham and Liz Nelson for their meticulous editing, to Jill Feron for her eye-catching cover and text designs, to Susan VanEtten for her superb photographs and art research, and to Katie Bull for her sales expertise.

Since the first edition, this has been a family project. I am indebted to my children, Jennifer, Sara, and Joe, who have contributed in many ways. I am grateful, too, for the editorial review of my sisters, Lynn Andrews Kotzen and Dale Andrews Eldridge, and my niece Debbie Kotzen. Thanks also to my nephew Daniel Eldridge, who designed the spiffy web sites for Concord Guides & Press.

Win Williams, editor of *SAR Magazine*, edited the spring 1997 article that served as the basis of the first edition. Jane Alexander, D. Michael Ryan, Vincent Kordack of the Boston National Historical Park, and Linda McConchie of the Freedom Trail Foundation kindly and carefully reviewed the text. Frequent helpful advice has been provided by Dale Szczeblowski and Kristie Johnson of the Concord Bookshop, Valerie Caragianes and Jim Hayden of Eastern National, and Charles Bahne, author of *The Complete Guide to Boston's Freedom Trail*. Eminent history professors at Brandeis University, David H. Fisher and Jonathan Sarna, have been very kind in offering me the benefit of their knowledge and perspective. My thanks also to Valerie Bessette for her excellent graphic design in the second edition.

National Park Service staffers have been helpful in many ways. They include: Nancy Nelson (superintendent), Lou Sideris (chief of interpretation), Douglas Sabin (historian), Mark Nichapor, and Clint Jackson, all at Minute Man National Historical Park; Kelley Fellner at Longfellow House National Historic Site in Cambridge; and ranger Dan Gagnon of Boston National Historical Park. I am thankful to many fellow Sons of the American Revolution (SAR) at both the state and national levels for their help and support. I also appreciate the more than eighty corporate, commercial, and institutional sponsors who helped me launch the first two editions of this book.

In Concord I am indebted to historians D. Michael Ryan, Tom Blanding, Judy Crockett, Jayne Gordon, and Tedd Osgood, as well as to my fellow

Concord Guides and fellow members of the Concord Historical Commission, Concord Historical Collaborative, Lexington-Concord Area Visitors Association, Concord Chamber of Commerce, Concord Museum, Orchard House, and The Old Manse. At the Concord Free Public Library I am particularly indebted to Marcia Moss and Leslie Wilson of Special Collections, director Barbara Powell, and Ray Gerke. In Lexington I have received invaluable assistance from Christine Ellis, George Comptois, and Skip Haywood of the Lexington Historical Society, the late Thomas Leavitt (director) and John Hamilton (curator) of the Museum of Our National Heritage, and Marcy Quill, director of the Lexington Chamber of Commerce.

Special thanks go to individuals who served as expert spokespersons for their towns' Revolutionary contributions: in Acton, Earle Nadeau of the Acton Minute Men and Betsy Conant of the Acton Historical Society; in Arlington, Lisa Welter of the Arlington Historical Society; in Bedford, Sharon McDonald of the Bedford Library; in Cambridge, Aurore Eaton of the Cambridge Historical Society and Kit Rollins of the Cambridge Historical Commission; and in Sudbury Guy LeBlanc and Richard Gnatowski of the Wayside Inn, Lee Swanson of the Sudbury Historical Society, and Carol Coutrier. In Boston I received assistance from Jennifer Tolpa at the Massachusetts Historical Society, Sara Leaf-Herman at the Freedom Trail Foundation, research coordinator Patrick Leahy of the Paul Revere House, and manager Renee Meyer of the Boston Tea Party Ship and Museum.

Finally and foremost, I am grateful to my co-authors, who contributed chapters about their areas of expertise. They are listed inside the back cover.

—Joseph L. Andrews, Jr., MD
Concord, Massachusetts, Autumn 2001

"Watching the Fight at Bunker Hill" (From Colonies and Nation *by Woodrow Wilson, originally published in* Harper's, *October 1901)*

For Jennifer, Sara, and Joe

For all the Paxtons, Kotzens, and Eldridges

And in loving memory of

My parents
Katherine New Andrews
Joseph Lyon Andrews

My wife
Margareta Langert Andrews

My sister
Ann Andrews Paxton

My uncle
Sidney New, Jr.

The Road to Rebellion in Boston, Lexington, and Concord

Statue of patriot Samuel Adams at Faneuil Hall. (Author)

Boston:
From Realm to Rebellion

★ ☆ ★ ☆ ★ ☆ ★ ☆ ★ ☆ ★ ☆ ★ ☆ ★ ☆ ★ ☆ ☆

Although modern skyscrapers tower above Boston today, the city is unique in America in that it still retains a great many original landmarks from its early history, dating from its founding in 1630. Fortuitously and often against great odds, these irreplaceable national treasures have been preserved and survive today, unlike those in many other American cities, where too many historical structures encountered wrecking balls rather than appreciative visitors. Traditional Boston neighborhoods closely associated with America's past, such as Beacon Hill and the North End, coexist with bustling modern Boston.

Bostonians—and visitors to Boston—don't just read about American history, they live side by side with it. Many still worship in colonial churches built when George III was king not only of England, but of Boston as well. Daily they walk past Boston's colonial and Revolutionary era buildings, such as Paul Revere's House and the Old North Church, on worn brick sidewalks along narrow, winding cobblestone streets. In Boston history is not dead. It surrounds you, informs you, and inspires you.

Boston first took root on a pear-shaped peninsula on the west side of a bay on the Atlantic Ocean. The Indians called the area Shawmut. The peninsula was washed by the Charles River to the west, the Mystic River to the north, and the Atlantic Ocean to the east. Originally three hills stood on the peninsula, which inspired another early name for the area—Trimount, an echo of which is heard in today's Tremont Street. The land was connected to the mainland by a narrow strand, later called Boston Neck. Starting in the late eighteenth century, the three hills were leveled, and their earth was used to fill in swamp areas to enlarge the land surface of Boston.

The first settler on this peninsula arrived in 1622. He was the Reverend William Blaxton, a minister. Two years after the Pilgrims had established the

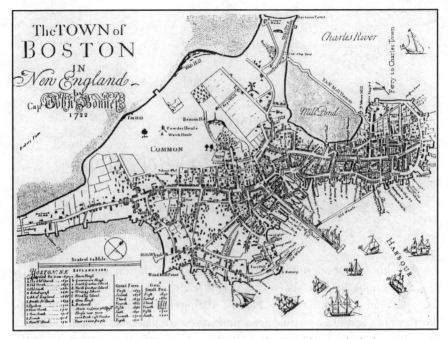

John Bonner's 1722 map of Boston shows the original peninsula on which the city grew. (New York Public Library)

first New England settlement in Plymouth, Blaxton moved to Shawmut and lived a hermit's life with his many books in a cottage near what would become the Boston Common.

In 1628 the New England Company was formed in London to settle in Salem, north of Boston. Its purpose was economic and religious, both to extend British mercantile activities and to find a hospitable haven to practice Puritanism. In 1629 a charter was granted by King Charles I to "the Governor and Company of the Massachusetts Bay in New England." This arrangement formed a basis for settlement and governance that would characterize the New England political landscape for the next 150 years: a British monarch granting a royal charter to a self-governing commonwealth led by a governor, initially elected by stockholders and later appointed by the king. (Morison)

In 1630 thirteen ships carried British colonists to New England. On June 12 the *Arbella*, carrying Governor John Winthrop and his Puritan followers, landed in Salem. Shortly thereafter, because of a food shortage, the ship sailed southward to what is present-day Charlestown, across the Mystic River from Shawmut. Learning of abundant springs near Reverend Blaxton's cottage, Governor Winthrop and many other Puritans moved south to Shawmut, which they renamed Boston in September 1630. The new community was named for a British town from which many of the settlers had come.

In Boston, Governor Winthrop and the Puritans set out to build a city according to Puritan religious principles, a "city upon a hill" that they hoped would exemplify Christian ideals in government and everyday life. The Puritans' buildings resembled those of the English towns they had left behind. Some can be visited today and are discussed more fully in the chapter on the Freedom Trail. The settlers purchased about fifty acres of land from Reverend Blaxton that became the Boston Common, used for grazing cattle and mustering militia. They built houses of wood, such as Paul Revere's House (1670s). Since religious freedom was a primary motive for the Puritans' migration, they constructed churches such as the Old South Meeting House (1669). King's Chapel (1688) and the Old North Church (or Christ Church, 1723) were Anglican churches built by parishioners loyal to the Church of England. Close to the churches they laid out burying grounds, such as those at the Granary (1630) and at Copps Hill (1660). Education was important to the Puritans; they built schools, the first being Boston Latin School (founded 1635, first schoolhouse built 1645). A year later they founded the first college in the new world, Harvard (1636), across the Charles River in Cambridge.

As ocean trade and fishing developed in the new port city, a complete infrastructure for seafaring emerged—wharves, rope works, sail works, shipyards, and warehouses. Shops for tradesmen such as carpenters and blacksmiths were established near the harbor. By the eighteenth century, Boston had become a hub of lucrative transatlantic trade. Boston ships transported fish, lumber, and rum to England, Europe, and the West Indies; sugar and molasses from the West Indies to New England and Europe; and slaves from West Africa to the West Indies and to the American seaboard.

Well into the eighteenth century, colonists in Massachusetts remained loyal to the English king. When England fought France in the French and Indian War (called the Seven Years' War in Europe, 1756–1763), most colonists sided with, and many fought alongside, British troops against the French, a common rival with territory in nearby Canada. They also fought against ideas that they distrusted: the papacy and absolute monarchy.

The colonists believed in "the rights of Englishmen." These rights, first articulated in the Magna Carta of 1215 and further developed through many subsequent political struggles, placed limits on the powers of British kings. Parliament, consisting of the elected House of Commons and the hereditary House of Lords, represented the people and set certain checks on the king's power. Along with personal rights, such as trial by jury, this balanced political structure protected England from both anarchy and tyranny. (Smith)

The government of Massachusetts, based in Boston, had a similarly balanced structure. After the second charter in 1692, the governor of

Massachusetts was appointed by and hence was loyal to England's king. Members of the Council, the upper house of the legislature, were appointed by the governor or nominated by the Assembly, the lower house. The Council typically consisted of wealthy merchants and the educated elite. Delegates to the Assembly were elected in town meetings to represent towns throughout Massachusetts. Together, the Council and the Assembly were referred to as the General Court. Each year the General Court and the governor met in the building now referred to as the Old State House (1713) to deliberate on matters relating to the whole province.

Although class differences were less rigid in America than in England, America was far from a classless society. Definite divisions existed among the colonial population, who were categorized as "the better sort"—wealthy merchants, professionals, and Crown appointees; the "middling sort"—shopkeepers, artisans, and farmers; and the "meaner sort"—laborers, seamen and slaves. (Smith)

The Council and the Assembly were clearly in the hands of the "better sort," the elite of the colony. Voting was a privilege extended only to one minority: white male property owners. Women, blacks, and the landless were excluded. Of the approximately fifteen thousand people in Boston in the 1760s, fewer than one third were eligible to vote. (In Britain, with a population of 8 million, 215,000 males, less than 3 percent of the population, were eligible to vote.) (Fleming) This inequity was the accepted fact on both sides of the Atlantic, and universal suffrage would be a long time coming. This left much of the population without a voice in government. Mob action was among the few ways in which the lower classes could make their opinions known.

★ GROWING UNREST ★

When George III became king in 1760 after the death of his father, George II, he was twenty-two years old and the first Hanoverian king to speak English without a foreign accent. (George I, born in Hanover, Germany, spoke only German and no English.) (Best) His accession to the throne brought the first troubles with the American colonists—troubles that would later multiply. Massachusetts customs officials applied for new Writs of Assistance when George III came to power. These writs were search warrants that gave customs inspectors the right to break into a home, shop, or warehouse to look for suspected smuggled goods. Colonists, and Bostonians in particular, had seldom observed these complicated laws, which were designed to maximize profits for the British government and merchants.

In 1761 James Otis, a Boston lawyer who had been convicting smugglers as a prosecutor in the colony's vice-admiralty court, resigned from his job to argue in court against these writs. He argued passionately that "the Writ is against the fundamental principle of laws." Because it involved arbitrary power, Otis stated, it was "destructive to English liberty," since any petty customs inspector could invade private property based on mere hearsay provided by an informer. American colonists took English liberty seriously.

In 1763 the Treaty of Paris, signed by England, France, and Spain, concluded the French and Indian War. The treaty ended 150 years of French rule in Canada, but its concessions divided England. Many of the English thought that George III had returned too many territories to Britain's traditional enemies, France and Spain.

Another huge problem faced the new king. The war had run up a burdensome national debt: over £133 million. George III planned to balance the deficit

The rights of Englishmen, guaranteed by the Magna Carta, were claimed in the inscription on a 1775 Massachusetts treasury note.

plus cover the costs of maintaining troops in America by taxing the colonies. This attempt to squeeze money from the colonists would have long-term consequence for the British Empire.

First, the Sugar Act was passed in 1764, giving new powers to customs inspectors to ensure that money would be collected from the importation of molasses from the French West Indies. Next, Parliament passed the Stamp Act in 1765, which added a new tax on the sale of newspapers, legal papers, licenses, and deeds. America reacted in anger to the Stamp Act. Led by Patrick Henry, the Virginia colony passed the Virginia Resolves, which supported the colonists' right to refuse "taxation without representation." In Boston, on August 14, 1765, mobs made their feelings known. The new stamp commissioner, Andrew Oliver, was hanged in effigy from the branches of an old elm tree, later called a liberty tree. When the sheriff arrived, he faced a mob of five thousand people, a third of Boston's population. The mob proceeded to Oliver's house, which they vandalized. The next day mobs attacked other homes of customs inspectors.

On August 26, 1765, mobs stormed the house of Thomas Hutchinson, the lieutenant governor and chief justice. They destroyed or stole all his furniture, clothing, and books. Boston's violent reaction to the Stamp Act ignited riots in other colonial cities as well, from New York to Charleston. A Stamp Act congress met in New York City in response to a call from Massachusetts, and

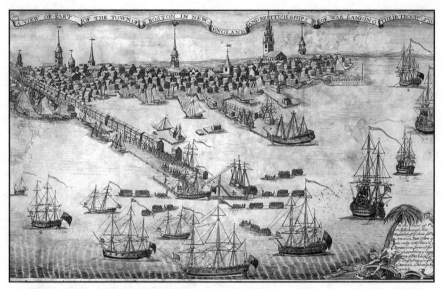

Paul Revere print of Royal Navy ships in Boston Harbor landing troops at Long Wharf, 1768. (American Antiquarian Society)

twenty-seven delegates attended. Their resolution stated their refusal to be taxed without their consent. They sent protests to London to the king, and to the Houses of Lords and Commons, accusing them of "subverting the rights and liberties of the colonies."

No tax commissioners remained to collect stamp taxes after the demonstrations. The colonists then declared that no ship could depart or enter American waters until the Stamp Act was repealed. These non-importation agreements were an early version of a trade boycott.

In London, Parliament summoned witnesses to testify as they debated the future of the Stamp Act. William Pitt, a British statesman and a friend of America, declared that "three millions of people so dead to all feelings of liberty as to voluntarily submit to being slaves would have been fit instruments to make slaves of the rest of us." Benjamin Franklin testified that enforcing the act would be both dangerous and costly to England. When the House of Commons voted in 1766, it repealed the Stamp Act. Colonists were euphoric about the vote, and the Sons of Liberty, a group of anti-royal patriots in Boston, led the celebrations.

However, just one year later, in 1766, Charles Townshend, the chancellor of the exchequer, proposed a new series of "extended taxes" on the colonies, called the Townshend Acts. (Townshend was also renowned as a drunken playboy, dubbed "champagne Charlie" by his peers.) The new taxes called for import duties on a variety of goods the colonists used daily—glass, paper, tea, lead, paints, and other items. Townshend also added a new system of vice-admiralty courts to enforce the new laws and stipulated that some of the new revenue would be used to pay the salaries of colonial governors. Thus the governors would be completely responsible to the Crown, not to the colonists. The Townshend Acts passed on June 29, 1767.

In Boston, Samuel Adams, a fiery leader of the Sons of Liberty, drafted an open letter called the Circular Letter, urging the colonies to boycott British goods until the taxes were repealed. Threats to the safety of customs commissioners made by the Sons of Liberty persuaded Governor Bernard in September 1768 to call in two regiments of British troops, about six hundred soldiers, to keep the peace. The presence of these British Regulars, often called "Redcoats" or "lobster backs" by the colonists, added to the tension between colonists and the Crown. After Boston mobs attacked the customs commissioner, General Thomas Gage arrived to take personal command of the British troops.

☆ THE BOSTON MASSACRE ☆

On March 5, 1770, Parliament repealed the Townshend Acts, except for a continuing tax on imported tea. However, on the same day in Boston a riot occurred, which inflamed the colonists far more than any tax levied by England. The "Boston Massacre" started when a young apprentice yelled insults at a British sentry who was guarding the Customs House. The sentry hit the boy with the butt of his musket and called out additional soldiers from the main guard. A large mob of about four hundred gathered and pelted the soldiers with snowballs. They were led by a tall mulatto, a runaway slave of mixed black and Native American blood, Crispus Attucks.

A member of the mob hit a soldier with his club, knocking him to the ground. When the soldier stood up, he was hit by another club. The soldier leveled his musket and pulled the trigger. Other Redcoats fired. When the smoke cleared, Crispus Attucks and four other colonists lay dead or dying, and six other men were wounded.

News of the Boston Massacre angered Bostonians as well as patriots throughout the colonies. Since the Sons of Liberty in Boston outnumbered the six hundred Redcoats five to one, a bloodbath seemed imminent. Lieutenant Governor Hutchinson was able to calm the situation by promising to arrest the errant soldiers and charge them with murder. But Hutchinson had a difficult time finding a lawyer brave enough to defend Captain Preston and his soldiers.

John Adams, a Boston lawyer originally from Braintree, Massachusetts, was persuaded to take the case. He believed idealistically that in a free country, legal counsel should be available to all—including British soldiers. Personally he had reservations about the violent tendencies of some of the Sons of Liberty, led by his cousin Samuel Adams. John Adams was able to seat a jury mostly of men from the countryside, who might take a low view of Boston brawlers. He found

Paul Revere's engraving of the Boston Massacre, 1770. (American Antiquarian Society)

witnesses who described Boston ruffians with clubs in their hands, looking for a fight with the Redcoats. Adams was able to portray the soldiers as acting in their own self-defense to protect themselves from a riotous mob. Of the six British soldiers defended by John Adams and and his fellow colonial attorney Josiah Quincy, four were found not guilty. Two were convicted of manslaughter and branded with an M on the thumb.

An engraving of the Boston Massacre by Paul Revere shows a line of Redcoats simultaneously firing their muskets at hapless colonists. Revere entitled it "Fruits of Arbitrary Power: The Bloody Massacre Perpetuated at King Street." The engraving further inflamed colonial tempers against the British occupying forces. The print helped create an image of British tyranny and American innocence that still shapes our perception of the event. (Fischer)

In London, Benjamin Franklin protested the presence of the British soldiers. He wrote that stationing a standing army in peacetime without the consent of representative assemblies was a grievance as great as Parliament's claim that it had the right to tax without the approval of those taxed.

In 1771 Thomas Hutchinson, formerly the lieutenant governor, was appointed royal governor by the king; his salary was to be paid by the Crown. This decision dismayed the patriots because it implied that the governor would not be accountable to the colonists.

Samuel Adams in 1772 conducted a Boston town meeting which formed the Committee of Correspondence, to communicate the "rights of colonists . . . with the infringements and violations thereof." James Otis was named chairman, and Samuel Adams and Dr. Joseph Warren, both Sons of Liberty, became active members. Their efforts promoted communication among groups of patriots in Massachusetts and throughout the other twelve colonies. (Fiore)

☆ THE BOSTON TEA PARTY ☆

In the spring of 1773, Parliament passed an act to end all import taxes on tea except for a tax of three pence per pound. The tax was meant to aid the British East India Company, which had a surplus of tea. The tax angered colonial merchants because it gave the favored British East India Company a monopoly on the import of tea and undercut Boston merchants who bought tea through middlemen or through smugglers who purchased tea in Holland. The tax also benefited the king's men in Boston, such as Governor Hutchinson's two sons, who as customs agents kept a percentage of the tea duties. Most other agents were forced to resign.

On December 16, 1773, a crowd of irate Bostonians met at the Old South Church. When the announcement was made that Governor Hutchinson had refused to let ships carrying East India Company tea return to England and insisted that the import duties be paid, Samuel Adams yelled, "I do not see what more Bostonians can do to save their country." As if on signal, a war whoop sounded at the door and was answered by another from the balcony. Yells went up. "Boston Harbor a teapot tonight!" "Hurrah for Griffin's Wharf!" Immediately several dozen colonists disguised as "Mohawks"—covered with blankets, their faces stained dark—left the church for Griffin's Wharf. They were followed by a large crowd of spectators. There they boarded the three tea ships. They hauled chests of tea from the holds to the decks, cracked them open with axes, and shoveled 342 chests of Ceylon and Darjeeling tea, worth nearly £10,000 into Boston Harbor. Thus did Boston men celebrate on a cold winter's night at the Boston Tea Party. (Labaree)

When news of the Tea Party reached London a month later, George III, Prime Minister Lord North, and the Parliament were enraged. To punish the colonists for such defiance, they pushed through legislation known as the Coercive Acts, often called the Intolerable Acts by the colonists. These acts (1) closed the port of Boston to all commerce; (2) annulled the Massachusetts Charter; (3) forbade town meetings—the glory of New England democracy, even as it existed under the monarchy—which henceforth could be held only with the governor's permission; (4) stipulated that the governor's council and all judges and local officials would now be appointed by the royal governor and paid from customs duties and thus made accountable (and kept loyal) to the Crown, not to the colonists; (5) provided that British soldiers and officials were to be tried outside of Massachusetts; and (6) quartered British soldiers in the homes of private citizens. The king and Parliament felt that the colonists would be intimidated by the Coercive Acts. Most were passed by huge majorities, up to four to one, in Parliament.

Lord North candidly explained the purpose of the Coercive Acts: "I propose in this bill to take the executive power from the democratic part of the government." (Fleming) Lord North also expressed the British attitude toward the colonists: "We must control them or submit to them." George III also often stated that he must subordinate the colonies to the royal will. Both king and Parliament believed they had the right to thus dominate American colonists.

Four regiments of British troops were then dispatched to Boston. The king appointed General Thomas Gage, commander-in-chief of the British Army in America, to become the new governor of Massachusetts.

Most of the men who made up the British army joined of their own free will, but at times forced enrollment, or conscription, became more common. One problem with the use of conscripted men was a high desertion rate. It is estimated that 10 percent of British soldiers deserted over the course of the war. Some British deserters were shot on the Boston Common in plain view of their comrades and the Boston public. This often added to the feeling of the Boston citizens that the British military men were cruel and heartless.

If Parliament thought that Bostonians would submit to the Coercive Acts without protest, they were wrong. Samuel Adams and the Sons of Liberty's Committee of Correspondence sent letters to the other colonies requesting help, and food was sent to the blockaded city from afar. The Boston town meeting resolved to "stop all importation from and exportation to Great Britain till the Act be repealed." (Fiore)

In May 1774 General Gage lost no time in laying down the law in Massachusetts. He nullified the election of councilors appointed by the Assembly. In September he sent two companies of Regulars to seize gunpowder stored by the colonists in a provincial powderhouse in Charlestown.

★ THE CONTINENTAL CONGRESS ★

To counter these measures, the General Court elected members to the Continental Congress to be held in Philadelphia. John Adams and Samuel Adams were among the five Massachusetts delegates. The Continental

A reenactor hurls tea from the Boston Tea Party ship into the Boston Harbor. (Author)

Congress, which included several representatives of each of the thirteen colonies, was the first effort by the colonists to put up a united front against England.

In September 1774 representatives of several towns in Suffolk County (which includes Boston) formally expressed their opposition to the recent acts of Parliament, stating "that no obedience is due from the province . . . that they [the Coercive Acts] should be rejected as the attempts of a wicked administration to enslave America." The Suffolk Resolves stated that the Coercive Acts were unconstitutional and that the compact between George III and the colonists was "totally annulled and vacated." This document resolved that no obedience to the Crown was due from any province. It called for sanctions against England, namely, an immediate halt to all trade between the colonies and England. It also called for colonists to form their own government and to organize militias for their defense. Copies of the Suffolk Resolves were carried by an express rider (courier), silversmith Paul Revere, to Philadelphia, where they were approved by the Continental Congress.

The contrast between General Gage and patriot Paul Revere epitomizes the struggle between England and America. For Gage, the rule of law meant absolute supremacy of king and Parliament over the colonies. For Paul Revere, it meant the right of freeborn people to be governed by laws of their own making. These basic differences fanned the flames of conflict between colonizers and colonists, creating the inferno of the American Revolution. (Fischer)

In September 1774 General Gage canceled the General Court, the Massachusetts legislature, after it met briefly in Salem. In response, delegates

John Hancock in Boston, 1765. Portrait by John Singleton Copley. (Museum of Fine Arts, Boston)

from Massachusetts towns gathered instead in October at Concord's First Parish Church to form their own First Provincial Congress. They met in defiance of General Gage, the Crown, and the Intolerable Acts, which banned public meetings without the permission of the governor. John Hancock was elected president of this congress. An executive committee of safety was formed, calling for companies of "militia Minute Men to hold themselves in readiness at a minutes warning, complete in arms and ammunition good and sufficient firelock, thirty rounds of powder and ball, pouch and knapsack." Every colonial town had a militia for its own self-defense. All men were required to muster several times each month to practice defense against outside forces, either Native American or British. The Minute Men were volunteers from the militia that could mobilize "at a minute's notice." They usually consisted of bachelors in their teens and twenties. (Galvin)

The Provincial Congress assigned Colonel James Barrett of Concord to collect and store military supplies—weapons, ammunition, tents, and food—for an army of up to fifteen thousand men. Concord was selected as the hiding place for supplies because of its central location and its supposed safe distance (about twenty miles) from Boston, where the entire British army in the province was quartered.

As 1775 dawned, the standoff between patriots and British authorities intensified. Clashes seemed inevitable. On January 20 William Pitt's proposal in Parliament to remove British troops from Boston was defeated overwhelmingly. On February 1 the Second Provincial Congress, meeting in Cambridge, urged colonial militias and Minute Men to drill more frequently and to procure weapons.

★ A STAND-OFF IN SALEM ★

On February 9, 1775, Parliament declared Massachusetts to be in a state of rebellion and asked the king to take steps to suppress the rebels and maintain

British sovereignty over the colonies. On February 26 General Gage sent a small force of Redcoats to seize military arms in Salem. Lieutenant Colonel Leslie and the Sixty-fourth Regiment were ordered to sail aboard a transport to Salem and seize twenty cannons. When they landed in nearby Marblehead and marched to Salem, they found that the local people had raised the drawbridge, thus blocking entry to the town. Leslie demanded that the bridge be lowered and ordered that British muskets be aimed at the colonists. This outraged the people of Salem, who told him that he had no right to fire on them without specific orders. They warned the British that if one soldier pulled the trigger, they would all be dead men.

Crowds began to assemble, forcing Leslie to compromise. When the drawbridge was lowered, Leslie and his Regulars were permitted to march over the bridge and advance thirty rods (about 165 yards) into Salem and then turn and return to their ship. Although Leslie captured no cannons, he could say that he had obeyed his orders. The story swept through the province, reinforcing the perception that British soldiers were not permitted to fire on colonists during excursions from their stronghold in Boston.

On March 30 Gage sent another expedition into the countryside, and militiamen followed them, showing the British army that the colonists could muster many militiamen who were not intimidated by the British soldiers.

Meanwhile in London, George III and his cabinet had a letter drafted and sent, telling General Gage that it was time to act to suppress rebellion among the colonists. Gage was to make the first move—to seize the leaders of the rebellion and their weapons—in a preemptive strike. The king's advisers believed it would be relatively easy to overcome the colonists if the British acted quickly. "A smaller force now . . . would be able to encounter them with a greater possibility of success."

The letter reached General Gage in Boston on April 16, 1775. He immediately began planning a decisive action—a march to Concord, to seize a hundred barrels of gunpowder, which his spies had reported were hidden there. Gage did not consider this as an act of war or an action that could trigger war. He felt his troops could march to Concord and back without firing a shot. If possible, he also wanted to seize the rebel leaders, Samuel Adams and John Hancock, who were staying in Lexington during the Second Provincial Congress in Concord.

In early April 1775, both the British and the colonists kept a careful watch on each other. Paul Revere, acting as courier for the patriots in Boston, rode to Concord on April 8, warning that the British Regulars would soon march to Concord. Tory spies reported Revere's ride to General Gage. Revere also rode to Lexington on April 16 to warn Samuel Adams and John Hancock that the Sons of Liberty in Boston had been watching British troop movements carefully. They discovered General Gage's order to relieve elite companies of light infantry and grenadiers from their regular duties. They also noticed that British ships in the harbor had launched longboats from the decks and moored them under the sterns, readied for rapid troop transport.

★ PAUL REVERE'S RIDE ★

On April 18 a stableboy ran to Paul Revere's house in Boston's North End to tell him that another stableboy had overheard British officers talk among themselves, saying that there would be "hell to pay tomorrow." Other alert Bostonians observed British officers congregating at the Long Wharf or learned from drunken sailors of orders to the navy. These patriots observed that British longboats had been rowed across the harbor from the HMS *Somerset*.

In fact, General Gage had ordered Lieutenant Colonel Francis Smith to muster approximately seven hundred men for a march from Boston to seize the Concord stores. Among the most elite British troops stationed in Boston, these men consisted mainly of grenadier and light infantry companies. Grenadiers were reputed to be fearless, large, and forbidding men, who wore tall bearskin caps. They were so named because earlier in the century, they had been equipped to hurl grenades, or small bombs, against the enemy. By the late eighteenth century, grenadiers had traded in grenades for muskets, but maintained their reputation as among the most fearless fighters in the British forces. The men of the light infantry, better known as the "Lights," were just

as fearless but were generally smaller in build. As "flankers," they patrolled each side of the main marching column to prevent attacks from either side. They often marched through trees and undergrowth; thus they needed to be nimble. (Cannon)

These movements were reported to Paul Revere and to Dr. Joseph Warren, a prominent Boston physician and a leader of the Sons of Liberty. Dr. Warren consulted a reliable informer to learn that Gage planned to seize Samuel Adams and John Hancock, who were known to be in Lexington, and then destroy the military stores in Concord. (Historian David H. Fischer specu-

Paul Revere in Boston, 1768. Portrait by John Singleton Copley. (Museum of Fine Arts, Boston)

lates that the informer was actually General Gage's American-born wife, Margaret Kemble Gage, a woman with divided loyalties to both her British husband and to her homeland. Historian D. Michael Ryan notes that orders to Colonel Smith made no mention of capturing Hancock or Adams and suggests that this entire episode may be more legend than history.)

Warren urged Revere to set off right away to warn John Hancock and Samuel Adams in Lexington and the militia and Minute Men in Concord that the British expedition was about to be launched. To be sure that at least one messenger reached Lexington without capture, Dr. Warren had assigned a second messenger, William Dawes, to take the overland route over Boston Neck to Lexington. Dawes was a tanner whose business often took him past the British checkpoint there, so he had a better chance of getting through.

Revere had a plan in place. If the British troops were to depart Boston by water, that is, by longboats over the Back Bay of the Charles River, his friends would signal with two lanterns. On the other hand, if the troops left by land, that is, over Boston Neck, they would signal with one lantern. All agreed that the signal light should be hung from the spire of Christ Church, also known as the Old North Church, then the tallest structure in Boston. At about 10:00 PM. Revere told the church sexton, Robert Newman, to hang two lanterns from the northern side of the steeple, so that they could be seen by patriots across the river in Charlestown, who would know British plans even if Revere was captured while crossing from Boston.

Across the river, patriots noted the two lights and immediately acted on the signal. They got a fast horse ready for Paul Revere and sent their own express rider westward to warn the towns from Cambridge to Concord. Paul Revere and two friends then set off in a longboat and started rowing north from Boston towards Charlestown. With muffled oars they slowly passed by the HMS *Somerset,* which was anchored in the harbor to block boat traffic between Boston and Charlestown.

Revere and his boatmen made it safely to Charlestown. There the Charlestown patriots gave him a fast saddle horse named Brown Beauty, belonging to Deacon Larkin. At about 11:00 P.M., according to Revere's account, he set off northwest towards Lexington.

Earlier that evening in Boston, General Gage had been setting his plan in motion. At about 10:00 P.M. approximately seven hundred British light infantry and grenadiers were awakened in their barracks and roused from their beds. They were ignorant of the objectives of their ordered march, since only a few officers, such as Colonel Francis Smith, the expedition's commander, were informed by the general that their destinations was Concord. The soldiers were told not to bring their knapsacks, but to carry one day's rations and thirty-six cartridges.

The Redcoats gathered at a beach on the edge of the Back Bay near the Boston Common. Twenty navy longboats awaited them for the trip across the water to Cambridge. The boats had to make two crossings to ferry all the Regulars across the river, taking up two valuable hours. More time was lost as Colonel Smith arranged light infantry and grenadier units to march through the Cambridge swamp near their landing site. Finally they were off on their march. The events that followed in Lexington and Concord would permanently change the relationship between the colonists and the British Empire.

✭ SOURCES ✭

Boston National Historical Park. *Trail Map.* Boston: 2001.

Fiore, Jordan. *Massachusetts in Ferment: The Coming of the American Revolution, A Chronological Survey, 1760-1775.* Boston: Bicentennial Commission, 1971.

Fleming, Thomas. *Liberty! The American Revolution.* New York: Viking, 1997.

Fischer, David H. *Paul Revere's Ride.* New York: Oxford, 1994.

Galvin, John R. *The Minute Men, The First Fight: Myths and Realities of the American Revolution.* Washington: Brassey's, 1989.

Ketchum, R. (editor). *The American Heritage Book of the Revolution.* New York: American Heritage Publishing Company, 1958.

Labaree, Benjamin. *Boston Tea Party, 1773: Catalyst for Revolution.* Boston: Todd, 1976.

McCullough, David. *John Adams.* New York: Simon & Schuster, 2001.

McDowell, Bart. *The Revolutionary War: America's Fight for Freedom.* Washington: National Geographic Society, 1967.

Morison, Samuel E. *The Oxford History of the American People.* New York: Oxford University Press, 1965.

Museum of Fine Arts. *Paul Revere's Boston, 1735-1818.* Boston: M.F.A., 1975.

Phillips, Kevin. *The Cousins' War: Religion, Politics & The Triumph of Anglo-America.* New York: Basic Books, 1999.

Revere, Paul. *Three Accounts of His Famous Ride.* Boston: Massachusetts Historical Society, 1976.

Scheer, George F. and Rankin, Hugh F. *Rebels and Redcoats.* New York: DaCapo, 1957.

Smith, Barbara and Susan Wilson. *Boston and the American Revolution.* Boston: National Park Service, 1998.

Tuchman, Barbara. *The First Salute: A View of the Revolution.* New York: Knopf, 1988.

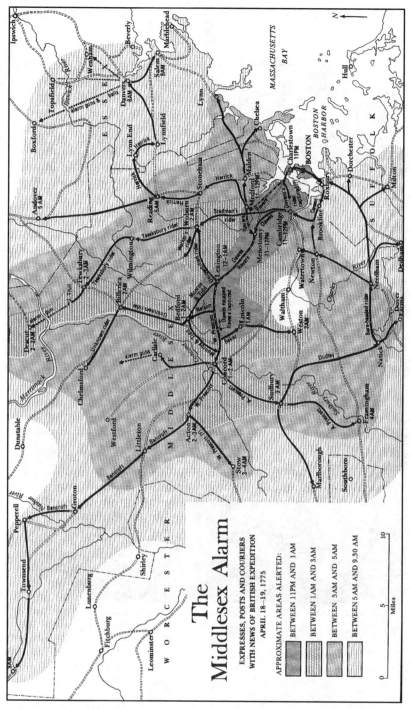

This map from Paul Revere's Ride *by* David H. Fischer *shows the many couriers who spread the alarm on April 18–19, 1775. (David Hackett Fischer)*

Paul Revere at Lexington (From Harper's Young People, *May 10, 1889)*

Lexington:
Where the Green Flowed Red

★ ☆ ★ ☆ ★ ☆ ★ ☆ ★ ☆ ★ ☆ ★ ☆ ★ ☆ ★ ☆

Paul Revere rode westward from Charlestown to Lexington. On his way he evaded a British patrol of two mounted officers. When he arrived at the parsonage of Rev. Jonas Clarke in Lexington at about midnight, he shouted to the militiaman guarding the house, Sgt. William Munroe, who told him not to make so much noise—people were trying to sleep.

"Noise!" Revere replied. "You'll have noise enough before long. The Regulars are coming out!" (He did *not* say "The British are coming," since in 1775 colonists still thought of themselves as British.) William Dawes arrived a half hour later. Both Dawes and Revere left Lexington and galloped westward toward Concord with the intent of warning Concordians that the Regulars were coming. Neither one of them reached Concord, however, as is detailed in the following chapters.

Some of the most dramatic events that plunged America into the Revolutionary War took place in a matter of minutes on April 19, 1775, on a small piece of land in Lexington then known as the Common and known today as the Green. In 1713 some citizens of Cambridge Farms had set aside one and a half acres of land next to the meetinghouse (church) for common land, which was later enlarged by one acre. The same year Cambridge Farms was incorporated as the town of Lexington. In 1775 the Common was merely a scrubby cow pasture in the center of town. The belfry bell summoned about 140 men from Captain John Parker's Lexington militia to the Common shortly after midnight on April 19. An hour later Captain Parker dismissed his men, and many retreated to Buckman Tavern for some liquid refreshment.

At about 4:30 A.M., when a scout reported to Captain Parker that columns of marching Redcoats were almost in Lexington, drummer boy William Diamond beat the alarm to recall the militiamen. Close to eighty men reassembled to form two rows on the northeast side of the triangular

This boulder on Lexington Green marks the position of the seventy-seven-man company of Minute Men during the clash of arms on April 19, 1775. The inscription is a quote attributed to Capt. John Parker. (Author)

Common. A boulder engraved with a musket and powder horn now marks the spot where Sergeant William Munroe's men mustered and formed the lines. These citizen-soldiers were a diverse lot: elderly Jonas Parker, Captain Parker's cousin; a black slave, Prince Estabrook; and teenagers William Diamond and Isaac Muzzy formed part of the ranks. All had been anxiously awaiting the British troops' arrival.

Now they suddenly faced an advance column of about two hundred British light infantry, led by Royal Marine Major John Pitcairn, who approached the Lexington Common from the southeast, having marched from Cambridge through Menotomy (Arlington). They were followed by about five hundred more marines, light infantry, and grenadiers, led by their portly, slow-moving, but experienced commander, Lt. Col. Francis Smith.

Parker did not want an armed confrontation between his small band and the over seven hundred British Regulars who were rapidly marching toward them; he merely wished to exercise the right to muster and "observe" the king's troops. To avoid any reckless gunfire that might have occurred by blocking the British column's route of march, Captain Parker first ordered his men, as Paul Revere overheard and stated in a later deposition, to "Let the troops pass by." Parker added, "Don't molest them, without they being first [to fire]."

One of his men, William Munroe, claimed almost fifty years after the event that he heard Captain Parker assert, "Stand your ground! Don't fire unless fired upon! But if they want to have a war, let it begin here!" This has become part of local mythology and is even engraved in stone on the Green. (Fischer)

Whether or not Captain Parker ever actually uttered this defiant challenge as the Regulars approached is a matter of speculation. Many modern historians doubt it. No other contemporary witnesses recorded these words, and it is unlikely that Captain Parker would have anticipated or desired an armed confrontation. All previous British expeditions into the countryside near Boston to intimidate the colonists (like that in Salem in February 1775) had concluded without gunfire. More likely, a veteran of the clash, with a less than perfect memory fifty years after the event, may have glorified his leader's statements. (Sideris)

The British vanguard was led by Marine Lieutenant Jesse Adair, an Irishman with a reputation as an aggressive officer. As he approached the triangular Lexington Common, with the more experienced superior officers Major Pitcairn and Lieutenant Colonel Smith riding behind, he had to make a quick decision. A large meeting house then stood on the easternmost angle of the Common (where the statue of the Lexington Minuteman stands today, still facing the direction from which the British approached). The road from Cambridge (today's Massachusetts Avenue) forked around both sides of the church. The left fork led west to Concord, and the right fork went northeast to Bedford.

Lieutenant Adair's snap decision was to take the right fork, the Bedford road, perhaps to avoid leaving the right flank of his column exposed to the assembled militia on the northeast portion of the Common, as he would have done had he chosen the Concord road. (Fischer) Thus, he led his column of three forward companies head-on toward the two lines of the assembled Lexington militiamen. (Fleming)

Major Pitcairn saw what was happening ahead of him and spurred his horse forward in a canter. Unlike Adair, Pitcairn elected to ride to the left around the church. Thus, he lost contact with his men and, more important, he lost command control of his forward troops, who marched rapidly out of his sight toward the waiting Lexington militia. (Galvin)

Militiamen, straining to see ahead through the dawn darkness, first saw Major Pitcairn appear on horseback on the Concord road side of the church, followed shortly by three other mounted British officers at full gallop. In depositions sworn just weeks after the battle, these militiamen testified that they heard the British officers yell conflicting orders: "Ye villains, ye rebels, disperse, damn you, disperse!" (testimony of Jonas Clarke); "Throw down your arms, ye villains, ye rebels!" (testimony of John Robbins); "Surrender!" "Surround them!" the British officers shouted above the din. (Fleming, Fischer, Sawtells)

Lexington's Captain Parker immediately turned to his men and issued them orders to comply with the demands of the British officers. As he later testified, "I immediately ordered our militia to *disperse* and not to fire." Most of the Lexington militiamen consequently turned and started to disperse, walking away from the oncoming British. No one, however, laid down his arms. Only two, Jonas Parker and Robert Munroe, remained on the line where they had mustered.

Lieutenant Adair, followed by two companies of light infantry, the Fourth and the Tenth, appeared to the expectant militiamen on the Bedford road side of the meetinghouse, immediately after Major Pitcairn and his fellow mounted officers had appeared on the Concord road side. On sighting the waiting militiamen, the British Regulars, completely out of contact with their superior officers and apparently believing a shot had been fired, lost control and started running haphazardly toward the colonists.

A shot rang out! Volleys followed from the muskets of the British Regulars, who then lowered their bayonets and charged into the colonial ranks. Eight colonists were killed and nine more were wounded. The rest fled through a thick cloud of musket smoke. The fierce cheer of British infantrymen rang out: "Huzzah! Huzzah! Huzzah!"

Who fired the first shot at Lexington? Over fifty surviving members of Parker's militia, in depositions taken within weeks of the battle, testified that the first gunfire did not come from *their* ranks. (Sawtells, Narrative, Fischer) Many front-line British Regulars later swore under oath that it did not come from *their* muskets. Did Major Pitcairn or Lieutenant Sutherlund, both on horseback, discharge their pistols first? Did a mysterious Lexington spectator fire from Buckman Tavern, as several witnesses later swore? Did both sides fire simultaneously? Were the first shots fired deliberately or discharged by accident? Unfortunately, we will never know. But we do know that the subsequent fusillade and bayoneting spree by the out-of-control British Regulars were deadly for the Lexington men, causing seventeen colonial casualties.

According to orator Edward Everett (1799), Jonas Parker, Captain John Parker's cousin, often had been heard to say prior to the clash that "be the consequences what they might, and let others do what they pleased, but he would never run from the enemy."

> He was as good as his word. Having loaded his musket, he placed his hat containing the ammunition on the ground in readiness for a second charge. At the second fire he was wounded and sunk upon his knees; and in this condition discharged his gun. While loading it again on his knees and striving in the agonies of death to redeem his pledge, Parker was transfixed by a bayonet and thus died on the spot where he first stood and fell. Like Parker, Robert Munroe was killed where he stood.

The rest of the slain Lexingtonians were killed while trying to disperse. Jonathan Harrington was mortally wounded only yards from his house on the Common, as his horrified wife and son watched. Bleeding profusely from a chest wound, he crawled to his front path and then died on his own doorstep.

One Regular, Sgt. Thomas Johnson, Tenth Light Infantry, was wounded (in the leg) in the Lexington clash. Two months later he would be mortally wounded at the Battle of Bunker Hill. (Fischer)

After the deadly encounter on the Common, Colonel Smith ordered a drummer boy to "beat to arms" in order to restore order and to call the Regulars back into formation. At about 5:30 A.M., the Redcoats continued their march to Concord, where they arrived at about 7:00 A.M.

✩ Revolutionary War Sites to Visit Today in Lexington ✩

Lexingtonians retain great pride in their unique Revolutionary history. Many original houses and several taverns, important in the events of 1775, still stand here. Knowlegeable local professionals and volunteers act as guides and offer a friendly welcome to visitors.

An excellent way to begin a visit to Lexington is to stop at the **Lexington Visitors Center** across from the Lexington Green. Information is available about historic houses and sites, most of them within a short walking distance. You'll also find information about local museums, restaurants, hotels, special exhibits, and historical and cultural programs. The gift shop features souvenirs and books relevant to Lexington's rich history. The Visitors Center is operated by the Lexington Chamber of Commerce.

Lexington today is a lively residential community of about thirty thousand people. Residents of Lexington and neighboring towns, along with visitors, arise early each Patriots' Day (usually celebrated on the Monday closest to April 19) to watch ceremonies on the Lexington Battle Green at 6:00 A.M. Modern reenactors playing the roles of militiamen and Redcoats face off across

Buckman Tavern (circa 1710). (Author)

Lexington Minuteman Statue, 1900, depicting Capt. John Parker. (Author)

the Green, reliving the historic confrontation of their forefathers. They fire musket "shots" at the opposing troops. After the smoke clears, slain patriots and Redcoats alike arise from their lifeless state on the ground, stand upright, and walk once more. Traditionally, churches and other organizations around townhost pancake breakfasts. In the afternoon, there is a town parade.

A visitor to the **Lexington Battle Green,** or town common, today will see many reminders of the 1775 conflict. **The statue of the Lexington Minuteman** stands guard by the entrance to the triangular Green and faces southeast toward Arlington, Cambridge, and Boston, the direction from which the British troop columns approached over two hundred years ago. Atop a rugged pile of granite boulders, the eight-foot six-inch greenish bronze man stands tall, a tribute to Captain John Parker. H. H. Kitson, a Boston sculptor, crafted the statue in 1900. "The famous continental [colonial] soldier is represented in a stern and expectant attitude, bareheaded and in short sleeves prepared to meet his fate in the cause of liberty. The old musket is clasped firmly in both hands, the whole figure representing strength and high purpose" (*Boston Globe,* on the occasion of the 1900 dedication). Historian D. Michael Ryan notes that few were bareheaded or in short sleeves at 5 A.M. on April 19, 1775. It was cold!

The contrast with another Minute Man statue, in Concord (by Daniel Chester French, 1875), is striking. French's Concord Minute Man carries his musket in his right hand, but his left hand rests on a plow handle, symbolizing clearly that he is a citizen-soldier, not a professional. Other Minute Man statues around the country include a second sculpted by H. H. Kitson (and his wife), which stands in Framingham, Massachusetts. Dedicated in 1905, it depicts a blacksmith with musket, hammer, and anvil.

Also on the Lexington Common (Battle Green) is a boulder with a plaque (placed by the Daughters of the American Revolution in 1910) marking the **site of the Old Belfry.** The belfry was originally built in 1761 atop nearby Belfry Hill and then moved down to the Common in 1768 to "hang ye Bell for Town's Use Forever." It stood next to the meetinghouse on the Common. A **reproduction of the Old Belfry** was built in 1910 and stands again on **Belfry Hill**, off Massachusetts Avenue and Clarke Street.

The **Revolutionary Battle Monument**, a granite obelisk on the west side of the Common, was erected in 1799 in memory of the Lexington men who fought and died here in 1775. In 1835 the remains of the slain Lexington militiamen were transferred from a common grave at the **Old Burying Ground** and deposited in a tomb to the rear of the monument.

The 1799 inscription by the Reverend Jonas Clarke lists the names of the slain men and asserts that the monument is

> Sacred to Liberty & The Rights of Mankind!!! The Freedom of Independence of America Sealed and Defended with the Blood of her Sons. The First Victims To The Sword of British Tyranny & Oppression. They rose as One Man to Revenge Their Brethren's Blood, And Defend Their Native Rights. They Nobly Dar'D to Be Free!!!

The Lexington Revolutionary Battle Monument has witnessed much more history. Beside it, France's Marquis de Lafayette, hero of both the American and French Revolutions, was welcomed to Lexington in 1824. The American centennial was celebrated here (and in Concord) in 1875. World War I soldiers were bid farewell here in 1917 and welcomed home again in 1919. Townspeople pledged themselves here to fight for liberty in World War II in 1942. And during the 1975 bicentennial celebration, thousands rededicated the Common and reaffirmed their belief in democracy. Ceremonies are held beside the monument each April on Patriots' Day.

The Lexington Historical Society owns the Hancock-Clarke House and the Munroe Tavern, and leases Buckman Tavern from the town. The society operates all three. Experienced guides conduct tours during regularly scheduled hours, and each house has its own gift shop. An entry fee is charged for each house.

At **Buckman Tavern** on April 19, 1775, the Lexington militiamen quaffed some flip and grog (alcoholic drinks) from about 1:30 A.M., when they were dismissed by Captain John Parker, until about 4:30 A.M., when they responded to William Diamond's drum roll and remustered on the Common, just prior to the appearance of the Regulars. Visitors enter the restored taproom, which has a great fireplace. Long muskets hang on the walls, and antique jugs, flip mugs, bottles, and loggerheads (heating irons) adorn the shelves. A costumed guide shows guests the kitchen, ladies' parlor, and landlord's bedroom—all furnished with authentic antiques.

The **Hancock-Clarke House**, one block from the Common at 36 Hancock Street, was built in about 1698. It was longtime home to the families of two ministers, the Reverend John Hancock (for fifty-four years) and the Reverend Jonas Clarke (for fifty years). Early on the morning of April 19, 1775, the arrival of first Paul Revere and then William Dawes roused Samuel Adams and John Hancock, the minister's grandson and a signer of the Declaration of Independence. They were staying there as representatives to the Second Provincial Congress in Concord. Forewarned of the imminent approach of the British, the two patriots were transported by coach to Woburn, then to Billerica, four miles away, where they joined Hancock's betrothed, Dorothy Quincy, for a repast of "cold salt pork and potatoes." The house exhibit includes William Diamond's drum and Major Pitcairn's captured pistols.

Munroe Tavern at 1332 Massachusetts Avenue, a mile east of the Battle Green, is also open to the public in season. Built in 1695, it was bought by Sergeant William Munroe in 1770. On the afternoon of April 19, 1775, General Hugh, Lord Percy's British relief brigade marched westward from Boston to Lexington with over one thousand reinforcements to relieve Lieutenant Colonel Francis Smith's embattled troops, who were fleeing eastward from Concord. Percy made the old hostelry his headquarters. Wounded Regulars were tended to there. Exhausted Redcoats rested and refreshed themselves at the tavern's expense. The British wantonly shot and killed John Raymond, a crippled man whom Sergeant Munroe had left in charge of his tavern, when Raymond attempted to flee. (The bullet hole remains in the barroom ceiling.) Besides the taproom, visitors can see relics of George Washington's visit to the tavern in 1789 and Sergeant Munroe's musket, as well as authentic period furniture, such as a four-poster bed and spinning wheels.

The Museum of Our National Heritage, on Route 2A (Marrett Road), presents changing exhibits about American history and culture and an ongoing exhibit entitled "Lexington Alarm'd!" which explores causes and consequences of the American Revolution. The museum and its library were built and are operated by the Scottish Rite Masonic Order and house permanent exhibits about the history of American fraternal orders, such as the Masons, to which many American Revolutionary officers and soldiers belonged. Entry is free.

Minute Man National Historical Park encompasses historic structures and landscapes in Lexington, Lincoln and Concord along the Battle Road, paralleling Route 2A. President Dwight Eisenhower, mindful of the approaching bicentennial of the Revolution, signed the law creating the park as a National Historic Site in 1959. It was made a National Historical Park (run by the National Park Service) in 1963. Currently over 1 million people visit the park each year. (See pages 48–51.)

★ Sources ★

Most of the sources referred to in this chapter are listed in detail after the Concord chapter. Other references specific to Lexington are:

Chamberlain, Samuel. *Lexington and Concord.* New York: Hastings House, 1976.

Fleming, Thomas. *Liberty! The American Revolution.* New York: Viking, 1997.

Lexington Historical Society. *Lexington: Birthplace of American Liberty.* Lexington: Lexington Historical Society, 1995.

———. *Three Lexington Landmarks.* Lexington: 1998.

Sideris, Lou (Chief of Interpretation, Minute Man National Historical Park, Lexington & Concord, Mass.). Personal communication, 1999.

Sileo, Thomas P. *History of the Lexington Battleground.* Acton: Concepts Unlimited, 1995.

Sterzin, Emily. *Lexington Battle Green: A Walking Guide.* Lexington: Lexington Historical Society, 1998.

Tourtellot, A. *Lexington and Concord: The Beginning of the War of the American Revolution.* (Originally published as *William Diamond's Drum.*) New York: Norton, 1959.

Who Fired the First Shots at Lexington?

★ ★ ★ ★ ★ ★ ★ ★ ★ ★ ★ ★ ★ ★

These conflicting sworn eyewitness accounts were given in depositions by both British soldiers and Lexington militia. Who did fire the first shot? Perhaps we will never know with certainty. This presentation was inspired by a permanent exhibit at the Museum of Our Natural Heritage in Lexington, "Let It Begin Here! Lexington and the Revolution."

★ WHAT THE PATRIOTS SAID ★

"Whilst our backs were turned on the troops, we were fired on by them, and a number of our men were instantly killed and wounded, not a gun was fired by any person in our company on the Regulars before they fired on us."
—Collective deposition of thirty-four Lexington militiamen, April 25, 1775

"I heard one of the Regulars, whom I took to be an officer, say, 'Damn them we will have them,' and immediately the Regulars shouted aloud, ran and fired on the Lexington Company, which did not fire a gun before the Regulars discharged them."
—Elijah Sanderson, Lexington bystander, April 19, 1775

"(I) ordered our militia to meet on the common in said Lexington, to consult what to do, and concluded not to be discovered nor meddle or make with said Regular troops (if they should approach) unless they should insult or molest us, and upon their sudden approach, I immediately ordered our militia to disperse and not to fire. Immediately said troops made their appearance and rushing furiously, fired upon and killed eight of our party, without receiving any provocation therefore from us."
—Captain John Parker, Lexington Minute Men, April 25, 1775

"The Second of [the British] officers fired a pistol towards the militia, as they were dispersing."
—The Reverend Jonas Clarke

"[T]he commanding officer of [the British] troops, as I took him, gave the command to the troops 'fire! fire! damn you fire!' and immediately they fired, before any of Captain Parker's company fired."
—William Draper, Middlesex militiaman, April 25, 1775

★ WHAT THE BRITISH SAID ★

"[O]n our coming near [the rebels] they fired one or two shots, upon which our Men without any orders rushed in upon them, fired and put 'em to flight."
—Lieutenant John Barker, Fourth Regiment, eyewitness account from his diary, *The British in Boston*

"Some of the rebels who jumped over the wall, fired four or five shott at the soldiers."
—Major John Pitcairn, Royal Marines

"3 shot were fired from a corner of a large house to the right of the Church."
—Lieutenant William Sutherland, Thirty-eighth Regiment, in a letter to Sir Henry Clinton, April 26, 1775

"[W]hen one of the rebels fired a shot, our soldiers returned the fire and killed about fourteen of them."
—Ensign De Berniere's report to General Gage on April 19, 1775

"Which party fired first I cannot exactly say."
—Lieutenant Edward Gould, Fourth Regiment, April 25, 1775

★ SOURCES ★

Fischer, David H. *Paul Revere's Ride*. Oxford, 1994.
Force, Peter. *American Archives: A Documentary History,* Volume II. Washington, 1839.
Kehoe, Vincent. *We Were There!* 1994.
Narrative of the Excursion and Ravages of the King's Troops with Depositions, Watertown, Mass., May 22, 1775. Reprinted by the New England & Virginia Company, 1998.
Sawtell, Clement. *The Nineteeth of April, 1775: A Collection of First Hand Accounts*. Lincoln, Massachusetts, 1968.

Concord's North Bridge, where colonial citizen-soldiers faced British Regulars at midmorning on April 19, 1775. (Susan VanEtten)

Concord:
The Shot Heard 'Round the World

★ ★ ★ ★ ★ ★ ★ ★ ★ ★ ★ ★ ★ ★ ★ ★ ★

An arched wooden span over the gently flowing Concord River was the site of the second interchange of gunshots between King George III's British Redcoats and the colonial citizen-soldiers on April 19, 1775. Colonists and British Regulars had exchanged musket fire earlier that morning on the Lexington Common, but there Captain Parker's Lexington militiamen dispersed, pursued by Redcoats. However, the Concord fight at the North Bridge represented, as the inscription carved into the marble of Concord's 1836 Battle Monument states, the first colonial "forcible resistance" to British imperial troops. (Ripley, French)

The first sign that conflict lay ahead occurred when Concord's Dr. Samuel Prescott galloped from Lexington into Concord Center at 2:00 A.M. to spread the alarm that seven hundred British Regulars had left Boston and indeed were marching toward Lexington and Concord, presumably to search for, seize, and destroy hidden colonial arms caches in Concord. Immediately after Dr. Prescott's arrival in Concord, the Town House bell was rung to alert Concord's militia and Minute Men to assemble. Two companies of Concord Minute Men and two of militia left their houses to gather at Wright Tavern.

They talked with their minister, the Reverend William Emerson (grandfather of Ralph Waldo Emerson), and agreed to send several "posts" (scouts) to gallop down the Bay Road toward Lexington to reconnoiter and get more detailed information about the advancing British forces. One such post, Reuben Brown, a harness and saddle maker, reached the Lexington Common just as the Regulars were arriving. As the firing began, he turned his horse and galloped back to Concord, without learning the details of the battle. When questioned by Major John Buttrick as to whether the Regulars were actually firing musket balls (not just exploding powder), he replied, "I do not know, but think it probable." Thus the fearful Concord citizen-soldiers did not know for certain what they might encounter as they waited for the British troops to

Concord Village in 1839 engraving from Historical Collections *by John W. Barber. (Concord Free Public Library)*

arrive in their village. Would the Redcoats try to scare them by firing blanks, or would they shoot to kill?

The men at Wright Tavern agreed that they should defend themselves, but not fire the first shot. Their Minute Men companies marched eastward, and about a mile from town they first spotted the frightening sight of a long column of about seven hundred Redcoats advancing rapidly, with muskets and bayonets "glistening" in the rising sun. They withdrew to a hill above the meetinghouse. The militant Reverend Emerson urged, "Let us stand our ground. If we die, let us die here!"

As the more numerous British forces continued their advance, the smaller band of colonials thought more rationally and agreed they should execute a strategic retreat. Colonel Barrett led them across the North Bridge to regroup on Punkatasset Hill, about a mile north of Concord Center.

After the British column arrived in the village, at about 7:00 A.M., British lieutenant colonel Smith and major John Pitcairn surveyed the town and the surrounding countryside through a spyglass from the Old Hill Burying Ground. Then they sent their troops in several directions. One company marched to secure the South Bridge over the Sudbury River to the east. Three companies were posted at North Bridge to protect it for the four companies who marched westward past the bridge two miles to Colonel Barrett's farm and mill; here Tory spies had previously reported that the townspeople had hidden some weapons and supplies. Since Paul Revere's April 8 warning ride to Concord, however, most of the military supplies had been moved from Colonel Barrett's farm to neighboring towns. Just before the Regulars reached the farm, Barrett's sons plowed the fields and hid the remaining weapons underground in the soil of fresh furrows.

The British search party entered Colonel Barrett's house and, finding nothing suspicious, went to the attic, "where the ammunition was actually hidden, under feathers for Mrs. Barrett's featherbed. She thrust her hands into the feathers and, giving them a flip, filled the air with down. The soldiers were so busy brushing the feathers from their fine uniforms that they searched no further." (Fenn)

The Concord and Lincoln men were now reinforced by companies of Minute Men and militia who had marched from Acton, Bedford, Carlisle, Westford, Chelmsford, Littleton, Stow, Groton, and other nearby towns. A force of about four hundred, they descended from Punkatasset Hill to a farm field (now called the Muster Field) directly above the North Bridge. There they formed ranks—Minute Men to the right (the place of honor) and militia to the left—facing the bridge. The British soldiers then retreated down the hill and crossed the bridge to the east bank of the Concord River.

Meanwhile, in the now almost deserted village center Colonel Smith's grenadiers systematically searched (without warrants) houses where they suspected weapons were being concealed. They searched the house of Lieutenant Joseph Hosmer, a cabinetmaker and leader of the more rebellious younger Concord men, who often argued against their most cautious elders. "They did not, however, discover the supply of ammunition because it was hidden beneath Hosmer's aged mother, as she lay in her feather bed. The family silver was tied to a rope and lowered into the well." (Fenn)

The British searchers did uncover three buried cannons, which they found by extracting the secret location from tavernkeeper Ephraim Jones. This was accomplished when Major Pitcairn held a pistol to Jones's head and threatened to use it. Under these circumstances Jones did talk and reluctantly revealed the hiding place of the guns.

To punish the defiant colonists the British soldiers, upon entering the town, had chopped down the Concord liberty pole and burned it. They later set fire to some wooden supplies and gun carriages, and flames accidentally spread to the Town House, setting its roof ablaze. An elderly Concord lady, Martha Moulton, pleaded with the Regulars to help douse the flames. They formed a bucket brigade and saved the building.

However, smoke from the burning roof, which billowed high above the village, conveyed a message that was to be misinterpreted by the colonial soldiers facing Redcoats at the North Bridge. The citizen-soldiers on the hill believed that the smoke they saw signified that the British troops were deliberately torching the buildings in the village of Concord center.

The colonists were enraged by what they thought to be the malicious attempt by the Redcoats to destroy their village. Lieutenant Joseph Hosmer challenged the cautious restraint of his superior officers by asking provocatively, "Will you let them burn the town down?" Colonel Barrett acquiesced to his men's anger.

The colonials quickly prepared for action. When asked by Colonel Barrett if his company would lead the march into town, Captain Isaac Davis of Acton drew his sword and replied, "I haven't a man who is afraid to go!" Colonel Barrett ordered his men to place shot in their muskets, but cautioned them to fire only if fired upon by the Regulars. Thus, as historian David Hackett Fischer points out, the strategies of the colonial officers at the Lexington Common at 5:00 A.M. and those at the North Bridge at 9:30 A.M. "were remarkably similar, to challenge the British force, but not to fire the first shot."

The provincial citizen-soldiers then marched down the hill to the North Bridge, reportedly to the fife and drum strains of the old Jacobite tune "The White Cockade." The Acton men, under Captain Isaac Davis, were placed up front, in large part because each had a musket with bayonet, whereas soldiers in other Minute Men and militia companies carried little of such equipment.

The Concord Fight is described graphically by historian Robert A. Gross:

> As the Americans advanced, the three British companies brashly crowded the east end of the bridge. Some Redcoats tried briefly to pull up the planks. When the Americans grew near, the British fired a few warning shots, then a direct volley. "Their balls," said Amos Barrett, "whistled well." Isaac Davis and his company's young Abner Hosmer, fell dead. Major John Buttrick leaped into the air shouting, "Fire, fellow soldiers, for God's sake, fire!" The cry of "Fire! Fire!" flew through the ranks from front to rear. The resulting discharge wounded nearly a dozen of the enemy (including four British officers). [One Regular was] killed immediately, and another died later after being whacked on the skull with an axe by a young American farmer. The British later claimed he—and others—had been scalped. However, these supposed atrocities had not actually taken place. [A third Redcoat died in Concord Center.]
>
> The provincials pressed on to cross the bridge; the British jammed together at the end, panicked and ran, unpursued to the town. The Concord Fight—"the shot heard round the world"—had actually taken a total of two to three minutes.

After crossing the bridge and regrouping behind a stone wall, some two hundred colonials still with Buttrick had an opportunity to fire at Colonel Smith's relief column and the four Redcoat companies as they returned from the Barrett farm, but they held their fire. The British marched back to

Meriam's Corner, where the "running skirmish" began. (Concord Free Public Library)

Concord Center to eat, drink, and tend to their wounded. After a total of four to five hours in Concord, at noon they began their retreat back to Boston.

The British retreat, also called the "running skirmish," began at Meriam's Corner a mile from Concord Center. The Regulars fought colonial snipers and small units from twenty-seven nearby towns along the sixteen-mile route of march. Fighting was particularly fierce in Lincoln and Menotomy (present-day Arlington), resulting in heavy casualties on both sides and stories of courage that still resound in local lore (see the chapters on Lincoln and Arlington). In fact, British forces might have faced total annihilation had they not been reinforced by over a thousand Regulars of Lord Percy's relief column, who marched from Boston and joined with their exhausted comrades in Lexington to create a formidable force seventeen hundred strong. Together, they fought their way back to Charlestown.

☆ REVOLUTIONARY WAR SITES TO VISIT TODAY IN CONCORD ☆

Visitors to the scene of the Concord Fight will arrive at the **Minute Man National Historical Park**, North Bridge Site, by foot, car, or bus. They will walk down a tree-shaded, stone-wall-lined path on the east bank toward the Concord River. The tranquil, green setting of field, forest, and meadow seems to belie the bloody events that occurred here.

The Concord Battle Monument, a twenty-five-foot granite obelisk erected in 1836, stands in front of the North Bridge. Its inscription commemorates "the first forcible resistance to British aggression." These words demonstrate that early Concordians were eager to differentiate the Concord Fight, where the colonials pursued the British and fired their muskets on order in anger and defiance, from the one in Lexington. At Lexington most of Captain Parker's militiamen, who were *dispersing* when the skirmish occurred, acted independently. (Ripley, French, Sawtell, Fischer) It is ironic (and a cause for heated debate) that this early American battle monument was constructed at the site where the "invading army"—the British—stood.

An engraved **stone marker** to the left of the Concord Battle Monument commemorates the two slain British soldiers who are buried here, Thomas Smith and Patrick Gray, with a eulogy by poet James Russell Lowell: "They came three thousand miles and died / To keep the past upon its throne."

The current **Old North Bridge** is a graceful wooden near-replica of the original that spanned the Concord River. Its center is arched and its sturdy railings invite you to lean at leisure, watch the slowly flowing water below, and enjoy the pastoral views beyond. The original bridge was removed in 1793, and the site was empty until a centennial bridge was constructed in 1875. The current bridge was built in 1956. While viewing the bucolic scene of the bridge and the tranquil river flowing below it, you can easily imagine yourself back in 1775.

Reenactors outside the Old Manse, built in 1770. (Author)

Over the bridge on the west bank of the Concord River stands the sculpture of the Minute Man, his left hand holding his plow and his right hand grasping his musket. The **Concord Minute Man statue** is the first major work sculpted by Concord's Daniel Chester French (1850–1931), who went on to create the imposing Lincoln Memorial statue in Washington, D.C. The Minute Man statue was unveiled in 1875 at the centennial celebration of the battle at the bridge, cheered by four thousand people including President Ulysses S. Grant and his cabinet. The inscription at the base is by Concord poet Ralph Waldo Emerson. Written in 1835, his "Concord Hymn" extolled the "shot heard 'round the world." Despite the continuing denials and consterna-

Concord's Hill Burying Ground, circa 1636, and St. Bernard's Church. (Author)

tion of another Middlesex town seven miles to the east, most readers interpret Emerson's "shot" as one fired from a musket at Concord's North Bridge.

A curving path up a gentle slope with a lovely vista of the river valley below leads to the **North Bridge Visitor Center** of the Minute Man National Historical Park. Within the original **Stedman Buttrick House** (1911) is a diorama of the battle, artifacts of historical interest, an audiovisual presentation, and a bookshop. Those who don't relish the hilly walk can drive there via Liberty Street from Monument Street.

Nearby is the **Old Manse**. Named by Nathaniel Hawthorne (*Manse* is the Scottish term for a minister's house), the house was constructed around 1770 by the Reverend William Emerson, Ralph Waldo Emerson's grandfather. The minister may well have viewed the North Bridge fight from a window in this house. Since the structure remained in the Emerson-Ripley family for almost 170 years, many of the furnishings are original, dating to the eighteenth century. The Old Manse is also famous as the house to which Nathaniel Hawthorne (1804–1864) took his bride, Sophia Peabody Hawthorne of Salem, to live from 1842 to 1845. Here he wrote his second collection of short stories, *Mosses from an Old Manse* (1846).

A logical next step would be a walk around **Concord Center** to enjoy its pre-Revolutionary and Revolutionary War ambiance, which still exists, amazingly little changed over the past two hundred years. Concord, called Musketaquid by the native Algonquian people, was first settled by recent immigrants from England in 1637, after they had purchased land "six myles square" from local Indians.

What is now **Concord Center** was originally built around the Mill Pond, which formed when a dam was built in the seventeenth century to block the Mill Brook. Water from the pond flowed over the Mill Dam to power a grist-mill. The British soldiers tossed the musket balls they confiscated on April 19, 1775, into the water of the Mill Pond. The still angry but ever frugal Concordians retrieved them from the water the next day. Main Street is still called The Milldam (or Mill Dam) by many tradition-loving Concordians.

At the head of Monument Square is the **Colonial Inn**, whose east end was built as a house by James Minot before 1716. The charming inn still accommodates guests and serves meals. Its comfortable bars and restaurant are popular rendezvous spots.

Old Hill Burying Ground (c. 1635) at Bedford Street and Lexington Road overlooks Monument Square. In use after Concord's earliest settlement, it was located next to the village's first meetinghouse (church). Concord's Revolutionary War leaders buried here include Colonel James Barrett and Major John Buttrick, the scout Reuben Brown, and Dr. John Cuming. The marble headstones are still well preserved and visitors can easily locate the graves of prominent colonial Concordians.

Wright Tavern (1747) still stands near Monument Square, at 8 Lexington Road. The Minute Men mustered here early on the morning of April 19, 1775. British officers used it as a headquarters, and later in the morning British troops gathered here to tend their wounded, rest, and eat before they retreated to Charlestown and Boston.

A short distance down Lexington Road, at number 20, stands the white-spired Church of Christ, or **First Parish Church** (1901). At this site, in a prior church building, the First Provincial Congress met in Concord in 1774, with John Hancock as president. It assigned Colonel James Barrett to supervise the collection and storage of supplies and weapons for an army of fifteen thousand men. It was with the goal of seizing and destroying this matériele that General Thomas Gage ordered his Regulars to march to Concord in April 1775. This congress also authorized the formation of volunteer companies to train and be ready to respond to any alarm at a minute's notice (thus the term *Minute Men*).

A historic stretch along Lexington Road, **"The American Mile" Historic District** boasts some of America's oldest houses. It comprises a row of clapboard colonial structures built in the seventeenth and eighteenth centuries. At that time Lexington Road was called the Bay Road, since it led some sixteen miles eastward to Boston on Massachusetts Bay. The road served as Concord's main street for almost two hundred years. After the demolition of the Mill Dam in the 1820s, what had been a causeway on top of the Mill Dam was

Orchard House, circa 1750, best known as the home of Louisa May Alcott and her father, Bronson Alcott. (The Orchard House)

rebuilt as Main Street. Many of the original houses on the Bay Road had shops on the ground floor and family living quarters on the second floor. Today most of these antique homes are privately owned and occupied:

The **Peter Bulkeley–Reuben Brown House** (early 1700s) at 77 Lexington Road originally belonged to the grandson of Concord's cofounder and first minister, Peter Bulkeley, and later to saddlemaker Reuben Brown, who served as scout on April 19, 1775, carrying the first news of the Redcoats' arrival in Lexington to his anxious comrades in Concord. Brown worked in his saddlery on the ground floor and lived with his family on the second story.

The **Concord Museum**, 200 Lexington Road, displays artifacts and furnishings from early Indian encampments and from Concord's early settlers; from Revolutionary times, including one of Paul Revere's lanterns and Revolutionary War muskets and powder horns; and from Concord's literary lights of the mid–nineteenth century, including Emerson, Thoreau, Alcott, and Hawthorne. "Why Concord?" is a six-gallery exhibition plus film and interpretive program, which explains why important historic and literary events occurred in the small village of Concord over many different eras.

The Wayside (c. 1714), 455 Lexington Road, is open to the public seasonally and is part of the Minute Man National Historical Park. Once (1769–1776) the home of Samuel Whitney, muster master of the Concord militia, it later became the home of reformer Bronson Alcott and his family, including daughter Louisa May, and still later to authors Nathaniel Hawthorne and then writer Harriett Lothrop (pen name Margaret Sidney). In

The Wayside (1717), home of Concord's Revolutionary muster master Samuel Whitney and later home to the Alcott and Hawthorne families. (Author)

September 2001, The Wayside was dedicated as a site of the newly established National Underground Railroad Network to Freedom. (The Alcotts hid at least one runaway slave.)

Orchard House (c. 1750), at 399 Lexington Road, was originally home to Concord's first lawyer, John Hoar. In 1676 he negotiated the ransom agreement for Mrs. Mary Rowlandson, the Lancaster minister's wife who had been captured and held by the Indians for fifteen months. Hoar's descendants were Revolutionary War soldiers, lawyers, and statesmen. Orchard House is most famous as the home of Louisa May Alcott (1832–1888), the author of *Little Women,* which is still popular today. She lived in this house from 1858 to 1877 with her father, Bronson Alcott, her mother, and two of her three sisters (her models for the sisters in *Little Women*). Orchard House is open to the public daily throughout the year.

At Meriam's Corner began the "running skirmish," the British retreat from Concord to Boston. The **John Meriam House** (c. 1700) at 34 Old Bedford Road is one of the oldest houses in Concord.

Colonel James Barrett's House (1705) at 448 Barrett's Mill Road was home to the leader of Concord's militia. It was used to hide munitions and supplies, making it one of the objectives of the British march to Concord on April 19, 1775. Today it is privately owned and not open to the public.

Concord observes Patriots' Day each year on the Monday closest to April 19. There is a 6:00 A.M. dawn salute with the bell of the First Parish Church announcing the arrival of a horseman portraying Dr. Samuel Prescott, who sounded the alarm that the Regulars were fast approaching. A parade features recreated units of Minute Men and militia from nearby towns and Redcoat companies; they provide a dramatic pageant at the North Bridge. There are also a call to arms and a twenty-one-gun salute near the North Bridge, led by the Concord Independent Battery (from their two horse-drawn cannons) and the Concord Minutemen.

The current company of Concord Minutemen was formed in 1962 to perpetuate the memory of the Concord soldiers of 1775 by participating in patriotic, civic, historical, and educational events, as reenactors and participants in "living history." In addition to ceremonial uniforms its members also wear colonial period dress and carry appropriate replica weapons and equipment.

★ SOURCES ★

Andrews, Joseph L. "Revolutionary Concord." Manchester: *New Hampshire Sunday News,* April 14, 1996

———. "Revolutionary Lexington and Concord: The Shots Heard Round The World!" Louisville: *S.A.R. Magazine,* Spring, 1997

Bradford, Charles H. *The Battle Road: Expedition to Lexington and Concord.* Boston: Eastern National, 2000.

Concord Chamber of Commerce. *The Lexington-Concord Battle Road: Hour by Hour Account, April 19, 1775.* Concord: 1976.

Concord Historical Commission. *Highlights of Concord's Historic Resources.* Concord: 1995.

Concord 1975 Celebration Committee. *Concord '75 Bicentennial Celebration.* Concord: 1975.

Fenn, Mary. *Old Houses of Concord.* Concord: D.A,R., 1974.

Fischer, David H. *Paul Revere's Ride.* New York: Oxford, 1994.

French, Allen. *Historic Concord and the Lexington Fight.* Concord: Concord Free Public Library, 1992.

Galvin, John R. The Minutemen-Their First Fight: Myths and Realities of the American Revolution. Washington: Brassey's, 1967 & 1989.

Gross, Robert. The Minutemen and Their World. New York: Hill and Wang, 1976.

Kehoe, Vincent J. The British Story of the Battle of Lexington and Concord on the Nineteenth of April, 1775. Los Angeles: Hale, 2000.

Minute Man National Historical Park. North Bridge Area Self-Guided Tour. Concord: Eastern National, 1999.

Revere, Paul. *Three Accounts of His Famous Ride.* Boston: Massachusetts Historical Society, 1976.

Ripley, Ezra. *A History of the Fight at Concord on the Nineteenth of April, 1775.* Concord: Atwill, 1832. (Reprinted by Acton Historical Society.)

Shattuck, Lemuel. *History of the Town of Concord.* Cambridge, Mass.: Folsom, 1832.

Soldiers, American. *Narrative of the Excursion and Ravages of the King's Troops And Their Depositions, April, 1775.* Concord: Eastern National, 1990.

Two Fateful Days in 1775, Hour by Hour

☆ ☆ ☆ ☆ ☆ ☆ ☆ ☆ ☆ ☆ ☆ ☆ ☆ ☆ ☆ ☆ ☆

T elling time in 1775 was an inexact science at best, so the following chronology of events on April 18 and 19, 1775, is approximate. Still, it helps to appreciate how quickly the rides of Revere and Dawes, the battles of Lexington and Concord, and the "running skirmish" unfolded.

☆ TUESDAY, APRIL 18, 1775 ☆

10:00 P.M.

On the orders of the British governor, General Thomas Gage, about seven hundred grenadiers and light infantry are awakened in Boston to carry out a secret march to Concord to search for and destroy hidden colonial weapons and supplies.

10:30 P.M.

In Boston, Dr. Joseph Warren alerts William Dawes, Jr., and Paul Revere about British troop movement. Dawes is dispatched on horse by land over Boston Neck to Lexington. Revere has two lanterns hung in the steeple of the Old North Church by sexton Robert Newman to notify patriots in Charlestown that the British will travel "by sea," i.e., across the river. British troops assemble on Boston Common, then embark by boats across the Back Bay of the Charles River to Cambridge.

11:00 P.M.

Revere arrives in Charlestown after being rowed across the Charles River. He leaves by horse and gallops toward Lexington to spread the alarm.

Old North Church. (Author)

MIDNIGHT

Revere arrives at the Hancock-Clarke parsonage in Lexington.

12:30 A.M.

Dawes arrives at the Hancock-Clarke parsonage. The Belfry Bell on the Lexington Common is rung, and about 130 Minute Men, under Captain John Parker, assemble on the Common. Dr. Samuel Prescott of Concord joins Revere and Dawes as they continue westward.

1:00 A.M.

In Lincoln, British officers on an advance patrol capture Revere. Dawes escapes to Lexington. Prescott jumps over a stone wall and escapes, then gallops westward to warn Concord that British troops are approaching.

2:00 A.M.

Prescott arrives in Concord, and the Town House bell is rung. Two companies of Concord Minute Men and two of militia gather at Wright Tavern. In Cambridge, British troops begin the march to Lexington.

2:30 A.M.

In Lincoln, Revere is released by the British patrol and sets out on foot to Lexington to warn John Hancock and Samuel Adams to leave the Hancock-Clarke parsonage. They eventually depart for safer quarters.

4:30 A.M.

In Lexington, a scout reports that the British Regulars are near. The drum is beat, and seventy-seven militiamen muster, then line up in a double row on Lexington Common.

5:00 A.M.

Major John Pitcairn's Redcoats face Captain John Parker's militia on Lexington Common. A single shot rings out! It is followed by a volley from the ranks of British soldiers. Eight colonists are killed and ten wounded. The first blood has been shed.

5:30 A.M.

British Regulars march from Lexington toward Concord.

7:00 A.M.

British troops arrive in Concord Center. Minute Men and militiamen withdraw.

7:30 A.M.

In Concord, Lieutenant Colonel Francis Smith orders three British companies to guard the North Bridge, four companies to march to Colonel James Barrett's farm to search for hidden weapons, and one company to hold the South Bridge.

8:00 A.M.

Redcoats arrive at the North Bridge in Concord to find that the colonials have withdrawn to Punkatasset Hill. Three British companies cross over the bridge to the west bank of the Concord River and set their guard.

8:30 A.M.

While burning wooden gun carriages, British grenadiers inadvertently set fire to the Town House in Concord Center

9:00 A.M.

Seeing smoke from the town center, colonials (who have moved from Punkatasset Hill to a field closer to the North Bridge) believe the British are torching Concord deliberately. They march down hill toward the bridge after Joseph Hosmer angrily asks, "Will you let them burn the town down?" British soldiers retreat over the bridge to the east bank of the Concord River.

Redcoat reenactors fire muskets.
(National Park Service, Minute Man
National Historical Park)

9:30 A.M.

Redcoats open fire across the North Bridge and kill two Minute Men, Captain Isaac Davis and Abner Hosmer, both from Acton. Major John Buttrick of Concord shouts, "Fire, fellow soldiers, for God's sake, fire!" The colonials advance and fire. Three British privates die and four officers are wounded. The British soldiers abruptly turn and flee toward Concord Center.

11:00 A.M.

British troops, including four companies from Barrett's farm, reassemble at Wright Tavern in Concord Center to rest and eat.

NOON

British troops leave Concord to march eastward towards Boston.

12:30 A.M.

Who fired first at Meriam's Corner in Concord remains uncertain. Here just after midday one thousand militia from neighboring towns begin their pursuit of the retreating Redcoats. The "running skirmish" has begun.

1:30 P.M.

The colonial soldiers, firing from behind cover of walls and trees, kill at least eight British soldiers at the "Bloody Angle" in Lincoln.

2:00 P.M.

At the border of Lincoln and Lexington, Captain John Parker's militia get their revenge by ambushing the retreating Redcoats.

3:00 P.M.

Having marched from Boston to Lexington with a thousand Redcoat rein-forcements, British general Hugh Lord Percy relieves Colonel Smith's exhausted men and fires cannons to slow the advancing colonials. Percy's and Smith's Regulars rest at Munroe Tavern.

5:30 P.M.

In Menotomy (Arlington) fierce fighting ensues between retreating Redcoats and pursuing colonials. Almost half of the day's casualties occur here, with many killed.

7:00 P.M.

Exhausted British troops stagger into Charlestown, having marched over forty miles in twenty-one hours with no sleep and little food or water and having endured constant hostile fire for over eight hours.

10:00 P.M.

Wounded British troops are ferried back to Boston.

AFTER MIDNIGHT

Other British troops return to Boston by boat.

★ THE TALLY ★

Seventy-three British soldiers are killed, 174 wounded, and 26 missing. Forty-nine colonials are reported killed, 41 are wounded, and 5 are missing. The Revolution has begun. Eight years of fighting lie ahead, to end finally with the American victory at Yorktown, Virginia, in 1781 and the signing of a peace treaty in Paris in 1783, in which England grants America's independence.

The Battle Road interpretive trail in Lincoln. (Author)

Developments at
Minute Man National Park
and the New Battle Road Trail

★ ★ ★ ★ ★ ★ ★ ★ ★ ★ ★ ★ ★ ★ ★ ★ ★

M inute Man National Historical Park in Lexington, Lincoln, and Concord has recently seen exciting new developments that will greatly enhance future visits to the park, increase understanding of the park's story, and strengthen connections between the park and local communities.

The park's Minute Man Visitors Center (formerly called Battle Road Visitor Center) on Route 2A at the Lincoln-Lexington town line has been completely renovated, with all new exhibits. One feature of the exhibit design is a specially commissioned forty-foot mural by artist John Rush, depicting colonists and British Redcoats fighting along the Battle Road.

The Minute Man Visitors Center also features a new multimedia theater program, "The Road to Revolution." This program, in one of the center's two theaters, educates visitors about the events of April 18–19, 1775, by the use of movies and videos, sequenced lighting of historic displays, an electric map of the Battle Road, and surround-sound narration and sound effects. Technology and media help tell the story of Paul Revere's ride from Boston and the Battles of Lexington and Concord. This exciting show is free.

The Battle Road Trail, a new 5.5-mile historical trail, connects points of interest in the park. This trail and its facilities (parking lots, restrooms, markers, and signage) greatly enhance the way visitors access and enjoy the park.

The main theme of the trail is the battle of April 19, 1775, which launched the American Revolution. In addition, the trail interprets natural history and the broader "human story" of the area. It tells about the people whose lives were altered by the events that took place here.

Much of the trail follows original remnants of the Battle Road. During construction of the trail, modern asphalt was removed and several sections of this historic "highway" were restored. Other sections of the trail leave the historic road to follow the route of the Minute Men, traversing farming fields,

Display at the visitors center at Minute Man National Historical Park, Lexington, showing a patriot courier. (Author)

wetlands, and forests. Before now, these components of the park had been mostly unknown by and inaccessible to visitors.

Park visitors can now walk, bicycle, or use a wheelchair to enjoy the entire trail or visit portions of it. Secondary trails in many areas allow walkers to loop back to the main trail. Because the Battle Road Trail is primarily an educational trail, it is not suitable for high-speed bicycling, and the loose stone dust surface will not accommodate in-line skating. Bicycles share the trail with pedestrians, wheelchairs, and children in strollers.

Granite obelisks mark the historic Battle Road, and low granite markers highlight the locations of historic houses. Locations of gravesites, where fallen British Redcoats were buried by local townspeople after the battle, are also marked.

The Paul Revere Capture Site in Lincoln (where the ceremony by the Lincoln Minute Men is performed each Patriots' Day weekend) has been newly landscaped and enhanced. Farm fields have been cleared and vistas improved, revealing a landscape approximating that of 1775.

As a global symbol of humanity's struggle for liberty, Minute Man National Historical Park attracts about 1 million visitors each year. These exciting new improvements will enable the park to more effectively fulfill its promise.

—Lou Sideris

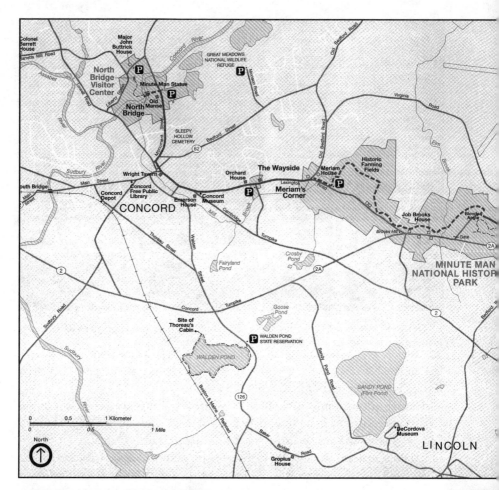

Minute Man National Historical Park *spans historic Lexington, Lincoln, and Concord and includes land around the original Battle Road. A mural by Chicago artist John Rush on display at the park (right) shows the so-called "running skirmish" between British Redcoats and colonial citizen-soldiers along the Battle Road on April 19, 1775. The site depicted is near present-day Nelson Road, just west of the Visitors' Center. At left are Park Service reenactors in front of the Lexington Minute Man Visitors' Center. (Map and mural courtesy of National Park Service, Minute Man National Historical Park. Photo by author)*

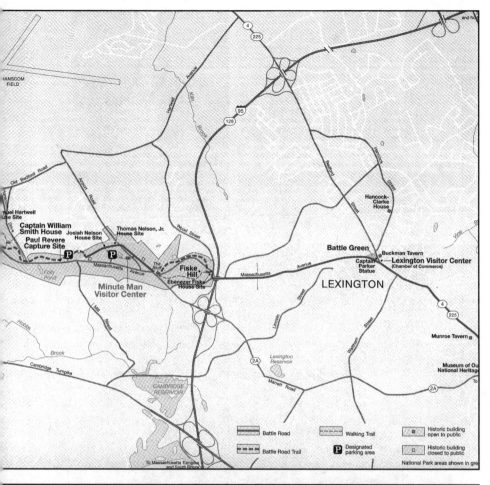

Statue of patriot hero Colonel William Prescott in front of Bunker Hill Monument, 1842. (Susan VanEtten)

Boston: From Bunker Hill to the British Evacuation

★ ★ ★ ★ ★ ★ ★ ★ ★ ★ ★ ★ ★ ★ ★ ★

Don't fire until you see the whites of their eyes" was the legendary advice given by a colonial leader at the momentous battle on Breed's Hill in Charlestown on June 17, 1775. (The colonials were low on powder; when the whites of the Redcoats' eyes could be seen, the British soldiers were close enough for colonial muskets, which had an effective range of fifty yards or less.) Some say these words were stated by Colonel William Prescott; others believe that Colonel Israel Putnam was their originator. Whoever said them, they have come to symbolize what is now popularly known as the Battle of Bunker Hill.

Immediately following the British debacles at Lexington and Concord, thousands of colonial Minute Men and militia, who had arrived in the area from all over New England, surrounded Boston peninsula and its five thousand occupying British troops under General Gage. This siege of Boston was to last for nine months, from April 19, 1775, to March 17, 1776. The provincials cut off all possible land transportation and escape routes, forcing the British to rely on the Royal Navy for supplies and reinforcements.

The approximately fifteen thousand men in the Colonial Army, under the command of Massachusetts general Artemas Ward, were a ragtag collection of loosely organized, minimally trained, and poorly equipped volunteers. Many of them, anxious to return to their farms for the spring planting, later defected before their enlistments were up.

To preempt a planned British attack on colonial troops surrounding Boston, in June 1775 the Massachusetts Committee of Safety secretly ordered colonial troops to fortify Bunker Hill, overlooking Boston Harbor. About twelve hundred volunteers from Massachusetts and Connecticut spent the night of June 16 not on Bunker Hill but on Breed's Hill, hastily digging with shovels to construct an earthen redoubt (fortification), 160 feet long by 80 feet wide, surrounded by walls 6 feet high and 1 foot thick and encircled by a deep ditch (moat) studded with fence rails and sticks. Although the Committee of Safety had originally ordered that the fort be built on the top of Bunker Hill, Israel Putnam, second brigadier general of all Connecticut forces, chose Breed's Hill instead because it was closer to Boston Harbor and thus more within the range of colonial cannons.

At daybreak, the watch of the British sloop *Lively* was astounded to see that a brand new fort had suddenly appeared overnight on the crest of the hill. British ships shelled it (with little effect). Enraged British officers met to plan immediate retaliation for the colonists' impudent affront to their dominance.

In the early afternoon, General Ward ordered additional colonial reinforcements. Two New Hampshire regiments, jointly commanded by Colonel John Stark, were put to work fortifying the Mystic River side of Breed's Hill.

The first assault at Breed's Hill by British major general William Howe's Regulars began at 3:30 P.M., following an amphibious landing. His troops had been ferried in longboats from Boston to Moulton's Point on the northern shore of the Mystic River in Charlestown. Angered by colonial sniper fire that harassed his troops, General Howe ordered that Charlestown be burned immediately in retribution. British cannons from across the harbor, on Boston's Copp's Hill, shelled Charlestown. The ensuing conflagration burned over three hundred Charlestown buildings to the ground as spectators watched from the roofs of Boston.

Redcoats attempted to breach wood fences and a stone wall, but were repulsed by the deadly musket fire of the New Hampshire defenders. At about 4 P.M., defenders repulsed a second British assault led by Brigadier General Robert Pigott directly against the colonial redoubt. The Regulars were hampered by carrying over one hundred pounds of equipment each, in eighty-degree heat. They were also slowed by attacking in field formations. Their scarlet uniforms made them easy targets.

However, the colonists' ammunition was soon almost expended, and they were outnumbered and exhausted from their all-night exertions. On their costly third assault, British soldiers cut through colonial defenses and overran the earthen fortification from three sides. The colonists abandoned the fort and retreated north toward Cambridge. After two hours of savage combat, British troops had taken control of the Breed's Hill fortification and pursued the colonists only as far as Bunker's Hill, where they dug in.

"Victory" for the British came with a stupendous price (as it always does in war). This bloody carnage cost them an estimated 1,054 casualties (207 men and 19 officers killed and 828 wounded), about 40 percent of their total force of 2,200 invaders. Marine Major Pitcairn, who had led the British columns to Lexington and Concord two months before, was killed. His son buried him.

"The Death of General Warren at the Battle of Bunker's Hill, 17 June 1775" by John Trumbull. (Yale University Art Gallery)

The estimated 2,500 to 4,000 colonists sustained fewer casualties (140 dead, 301 wounded and 30 taken prisoner) (Fleming). But a grave loss was the death of Dr. Joseph Warren, physician, patriot leader, and brave soldier.

Despite the fact that the British ousted the patriots from Breed's Hill, the battle came to be viewed as a type of success for the colonists. It is remembered as such today. In the words of historian Thomas Fleming:

> Only gradually did colonists begin to see Bunker Hill as a kind of victory. One of the first to reach this conclusion was a young Rhode Island general, Nathaniel Greene: "I wish we could sell them another hill at the same price," he said. Today we know that the battle crippled the British Army and threw it on the defensive for more than a year.

Three weeks after the Battle of Bunker Hill, on July 3, 1775, General George Washington arrived in Cambridge to take command of the newly designated Continental Army. He found a collection of militiamen from different towns, mostly from New England, who were ill-trained, ill-equipped, and ill-disciplined. But these were the men that he was assigned not only to train but also to command in the siege of Boston.

The colonial troops formed an eight-mile semicircle of fortifications to surround the British troops, which were confined to the Boston and Charlestown peninsulas—cut off by land but supplied by sea by the powerful British navy. The British had heavily fortified Bunker Hill, Boston Neck, and the shore of the Back Bay to defend their positions.

The colonists lacked the artillery for an assault to break this stalemate, and they were short of gunpowder. Many defectors from the colonial side returned to their homes. Many colonists with patriotic sympathies had abandoned Boston, leaving it mainly to British troops and loyalists. Paul Revere, for example, took his family to Watertown to wait out the siege.

Washington, fighting a huge morale problem due to the stalemate, favored an all-out assault over Boston Neck and across the Back Bay to destroy the occupying British army. However, he was unable to persuade his fellow generals to follow this plan. Even though George III had made a proclamation of rebellion in August 1775, asserting that his colonies were "traitorously waging war" against the Crown and calling for "suppression of the rebellion," many colonial officers and members of the Continental Congress still hoped for reconciliation. Washington, however, after learning the details of Bunker Hill at his arrival in Boston, had become convinced that it was time "to shake off all connections with a state so unjust and unnatural." (Fleming)

In December 1775, Washington assigned a seemingly impossible mission to Henry Knox, a bookseller turned artillery officer. Knox was sent to Fort Ticonderoga in New York to transport captured British cannons over a distance of 250 miles eastward to Boston. The cannons had been floated down Lake George from Lake Champlain. On December 24, sixty tons of artillery were loaded on sledges, which were pulled by oxen over rutted roads, ice, and snowy hills, and through woods and over rivers. The fifty-nine iron cannons weighed from 100 to 5,500 pounds each. The "Knox Trail" passed by Albany, Springfield, and Worcester. The cannons arrived in the vicinity of Boston on January 24, 1776. On March 4 they were secretly hauled up to Dorchester Heights, overlooking Boston Harbor, a Herculean task requiring two thousand men and four hundred oxen. The colonists also built six earthen forts to protect the cannons. The next morning the British awoke to stare in disbelief at what the colonists had constructed overnight. Colonial cannons commanded Boston Harbor and the British fleet.

Washington had drawn up an intricate plan for attacking Boston. British general William Howe soon had his own elaborate plan to attack colonial lines and seize the cannons in Dorchester. "The stage was set for a titanic showdown." (Fleming)

However, as darkness fell on the evening of March 5, a violent storm with wind, snow, and hail hit Boston from the south. General Howe's chief engineer persuaded him that the risk of trying to assault Dorchester Heights during the storm would be worse than attacking Bunker Hill. Howe announced that "the badness of the weather" forced him to cancel the attack. He also ordered working parties to load the Royal Navy ships as swiftly as possible.

The British toiled day and night to load their baggage, stores, and ammunition aboard the ships. More than a thousand loyalists prepared to board them as well, to leave Boston for New York City or northeastern Canada. Washington kept his guns silent, perhaps because of the pleas of Boston selectmen who urged him not to fire on the city.

On Sunday morning, March 17, 1776, the British fleet sailed out of Boston Harbor with the entire British army and their loyalist followers. Today on each March 17 in Boston, there are *two* celebrations—St. Patrick's Day and Evacuation Day, the day the British left Boston, never to return.

✯ SOURCES ✯

Sources for this chapter are the same as for the first chapter on Boston, with these additions:

Boston National Historic Park. *Bunker Hill.* Boston: National Park Service, 2000.

Jennings, John. *Boston: Cradle of Liberty, 1630-1776.* New York: Doubleday, 1947.

Russell, Francis. *Lexington, Concord and Bunker Hill.* New York: American Heritage, 1963.

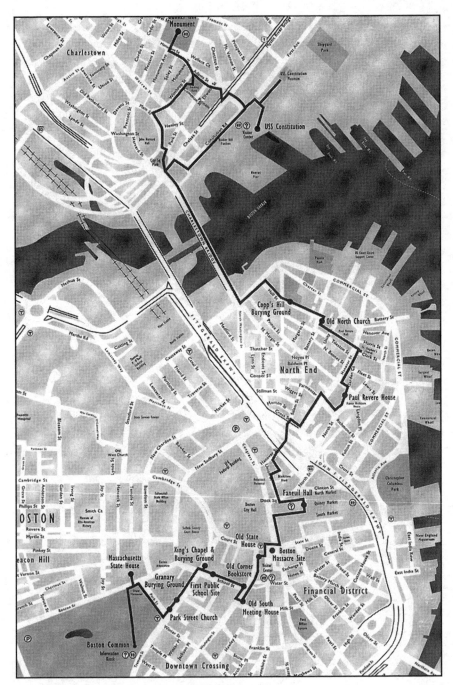

Map of the Freedom Trail. (Freedom Trail Foundation)

The Freedom Trail:
A Walk Through Boston's Past

★ ★ ★ ★ ★ ★ ★ ★ ★ ★ ★ ★ ★ ★ ★ ★ ★

The Freedom Trail is one of the most popular destinations for visitors to Boston. That said, it might be helpful to start with what the Freedom Trail is *not*. It is *not* a theme park like Disney World. "The sites along the Freedom Trail are not re-creations or adaptations. They are *real*. Each has its own special role in the beginning of a nation," states the Freedom Trail Foundation.

The Freedom Trail is *not* a living re-enactment like Colonial Williamsburg or Plimouth Plantation, which are historical re-creations, set apart from everyday life. The Freedom Trail winds through the heart of today's Boston and across the Charles River to Charlestown, letting visitors see remnants of the past amid the hustle and bustle of contemporary life.

It is *not* a path that can be viewed in less than an hour. To do justice to all the sites on the trail will require half a day to one full day, or for Boston area residents, many days done gradually over many years. It *cannot* be covered in a car. Because of narrow, winding, one-way streets, it can be covered only on foot.

What then *is* the Freedom Trail? It is a 2.5-mile path, starting at the Boston Common and winding past sixteen of Boston's major historic sites to end at Bunker Hill in Charlestown across the Charles River. A red brick (or red painted) line on the sidewalk leads to independent sites located in neighborhoods associated with different eras and historic events. Walkers can experience "Old Boston": Puritan and colonial Boston of the seventeenth century, Revolutionary War Boston of the eighteenth century, and Federal Boston of the early nineteenth century. The trail passes through a variety of ethnic and cultural enclaves, such as Brahmin Beacon Hill, commercial Downtown Crossing, touristy Quincy Market, the Italian North End, and Irish Charlestown.

National Park Service ranger on the Freedom Trail. (Susan VanEtten)

The idea of the Freedom Trail originated with a Boston newspaperman, William G. Schofield, in 1951. In his delightful book *Freedom by the Bay,* he explains that "tourists were going berserk in those days, bumbling around and frothing at the mouth, because they couldn't find what they were looking for. It was not unusual for a safari trying to track down Faneuil Hall to get lost in the tattoo shops and burlesque dives of old Scollay Square. . . . It was chaos. The obvious solution was to link the sites in numbered sequence along a clearly marked and charted trail, so that a visitor might follow the route from end to end without ever arriving at a wrong door."

It made sense then, as it does now, that the trail should follow the routes that hundreds of Boston colonials would have walked in their daily eighteenth-century activities . . . across Boston Common . . . past King's Chapel . . . to the Faneuil Hall Market Place . . . or the Old South Meeting House. It was directly along these routes that the major events took place that led to the birth of American freedom.

Today the Freedom Trail is supported by a collaboration of independent groups that manage the sites, together with the assistance of the National Park Service, the Freedom Trail Foundation, the Greater Boston Convention and Visitors Bureau, and other organizations. The trail overlaps with the Boston Historical Park, "an association of a number of sites that together provide a coherent view of the nation's history. Each site brings to life the American ideals of freedom of speech, religion, government and self-determination." It is a cooperative venture involving the city of Boston, private owners, and the federal government, which owns only three of the sites.

When I last visited the Old South Meeting House on a cold winter's day, a young couple asked out loud, to no one in particular, "Why should we be visiting this place? What happened here?" I took it upon myself to explain to them the excitement of Sam Adams's revolutionary rhetoric at the Old South, especially just before the Boston Tea Party held on a cold December day in 1773. This chapter (and others in the book) aim to answer such basic questions—what is special about each major site and why is it worth a visit.

To get the most out of your visit to the Freedom Trail:

1. Bring a good guidebook (like this one) to keep you on course in the maze of Boston's winding streets.

2. Stop at the Visitor Information Center on the Boston Common on Tremont Street or at the National Park Service Visitors Center at 15 State Street opposite the Old State House.* You'll find maps, brochures, exhibits, and the latest information about special events and guided tours.

3. Consider taking a guided tour. National Park rangers lead ninety-minute guided tours daily in season from April to September. They leave from the State Street Visitors Center hourly from 10:00 A.M. to 3:00 P.M. Rangers also present historical talks at Faneuil Hall daily, at every half hour from 9:00 A.M. to 5:00 P.M. Walking tours led by costumed guides are also available with the Freedom Trail Players. Boston by Foot provides guided walking tours to many parts of Boston. Several bus and "trolley" tours will drop you off near the historic sites and permit you to disembark and reboard at will throughout the day, without additional charges.

4. Consider breaking your Freedom Trail visit into small segments, to accommodate family members' different interests and tolerance for walking. You might pace your visits over several days. For example, if you are interested in history and government, you may spend over an hour in the State House, one hour in the Old South Meeting House, and a third hour in Faneuil Hall. Then rest and eat at one of the many excellent restaurants at Quincy Market or in the North End.

5. Consider different transportation options. You might park the car all day in a garage such as the Boston Common underground garage. Walk or take public transit, the "T," to visit sites in different parts of the city. For those unfamiliar with Boston, the many one-way streets can make driving a nuisance.

6. Let your imagination go. You will be at the actual places where unique American historic events happened. Try to imagine yourself being there then, and don't be afraid to get excited by the experience. Learn . . . and return.

✭ THE BOSTON COMMON ✭

The Freedom Trail starts* at the Boston Common, which consists of forty-four acres of open green space in the middle of Boston. It initially served as pastureland for Boston's first settler, the hermit minister William Blaxton, who arrived in 1622. At the time the peninsula was called Shawmut, the Algonquian term for "living waters."

---

* Because of better (and cheaper) parking, many visitors now "begin at the end" of the Freedom Trail, starting at the National Park Service Visitor Center outside Gate 1 of the Charlestown Navy Yard.

Puritan settlers moved to the peninsula in 1630. In 1634 they paid Blaxton £30 to purchase the common land, which they wanted to use for "the feeding of cattell and for a trayning field for militia."

In the mid-1600s the Common became a town dump, but the town fathers passed a law in 1652 to forbid the dumping of dead animals and garbage there. During Puritan times, the Common was witness to a fascinating succession of events that included the strangling of pirates, the garroting of Quakers, the hanging of witches, the stoning of Catholics, the baiting of bears, the fighting of duels, the beating of slaves, the caging of Sabbath breakers, and the drenching of sinners by means of a ducking stool overhanging the Frog Pond, which today contains no frogs. (Schofield)

During the British occupation of Boston in the 1770s, British troops set up their tents and trained on the Common. On the evening of April 18, 1775, about seven hundred British Redcoats assembled here. Then, led by Lieutenant Colonel Francis Smith and Major John Pitcairn, they embarked from a spot near today's Public Gardens at Charles Street and Boylston Street, which, before landfill built up the area, was situated at the water's edge by the Back Bay of the Charles River. The Redcoats were ferried by longboats across the Back Bay to Lechmere Point in Cambridge to begin their twenty-four hour ordeal of marching westward to Lexington and Concord and then eastward in rapid retreat from Concord, back to Boston, after the unexpected battles at Lexington and Concord.

Boston Common with Boston's financial district in the distance. (Author)

Statue of George Washington at the State House. (Author)

The Common is still a central place in the lives of Bostonians. In the forty years that I have lived in the Boston area, I have seen: anti-Vietnam War rallies (the air heavy with scent of the weed), one of Judy Garland's last concerts, an appearance by the pope, late-afternoon meetings of dog owners and running dogs, dairy cattle milking demonstrations, arts festivals, and parents wheeling kids in strollers. (When we lived on Beacon Hill with an infant, we considered the Common our "back yard.") In the winter well-bundled Bostonians lean against the cold wind that whips over the Common, scurry across the snowy paths to work, ice-skate at the Frog Pond, and sled on the hills. During every season, lovers hold hands.

☆ THE "NEW" MASSACHUSETTS STATE HOUSE ☆

Along the red line marking the Freedom Trail from the Boston Common Visitors Center on Tremont Street, it's an easy uphill walk to the Massachusetts State House, clearly recognizable with its shining golden dome.

The "Old" State House had been home to the Massachusetts legislature under the British since 1713. After independence, citizens wanted a new capital building. In 1795 the cornerstone for the "New" State House was laid, after being pulled uphill by fifteen horses symbolizing all the states in the Union. Governor Samuel Adams and Paul Revere officiated. The architect was Charles Bulfinch, a Bostonian who also helped design the U.S. Capitol. The land was adjacent to the mansion of wealthy merchant John Hancock, first governor of the Commonwealth.

Three years later the new state capital building was complete, though it had far exceeded its budget. The dome was originally covered with wooden shingles, which proved to be leaky. So in 1802 Paul Revere's company clad the dome in copper. It was first given its characteristic gilding after the Civil War. Mid-nineteenth-century engravings of Boston show the gold-domed State House as the tallest structure in Boston, crowning Beacon Hill. It would have stood even higher, except that, in preceding years, the height of Beacon Hill had been reduced by sixty feet. Its dirt had been carted away to fill in the Mill Pond.

A quick look-see at the State House might take ten minutes. A full tour with a well-informed volunteer guide, a Doric Dame, could take well over an hour. Entry is through doors to the right when facing the front of the building. (Only a departing governor or a visiting president is permitted to use the center doors.)

The building's series of elegant halls begins with Doric Hall, named for its tall doric columns; this reception room is the setting for many state functions. Nurses Hall commemorates Civil War nurses. The Hall of Flags displays more than four hundred Massachusetts regimental flags representing some of the state units that have served in combat in many different wars, including the American Revolution. Large murals illustrate events in state history, including the Pilgrims' arrival on the *Mayflower* in 1620 and the Battle at Concord in 1775. The Great Hall, completed in 1990, displays flags from each of the 351 cities and towns in Massachusetts.

From the sweeping marble main staircase that ascends to the third floor, the inside of the Senate Chambers can be glimpsed. The desks of the forty state senators are arranged in a circle. The larger House Chambers, occupied

Chambers of the Massachusetts General Court, the state's house of representatives. (Susan VanEtten)

by the 160 state representatives, is distinguished by the Sacred Cod, a wooden fish that hangs overhead. Symbolizing the importance of the fishing industry to the state economy, it was originally donated by merchant John Rowe in 1784. Historic murals line both chambers. Executive offices of the governor, cabinet, and governor's council are also on the third floor.

The grounds of the State House include several statues portraying important figures in Massachusetts history, such as orator Daniel Webster, educator Horace Mann, and Civil War general Joseph Hooker, astride his horse. The most recent addition, in 1990, is a statue of President John F. Kennedy. Less than positive moments in state history are

The Great Hall of the Massachusetts State House. (Susan VanEtten)

represented by statues of colonial religious dissidents. Mary Dwyer, a Quaker, was hanged on Boston Common in 1660. Anne Hutchinson, an independent thinker whose influence over several colonists appeared threatening to the religious and civic leaders of her day, was excommunicated by Puritan ministers and then exiled from the state in 1637.

☆ BEACON HILL ☆

While not officially part of the Freedom Trail, Beacon Hill is well worth a stroll at some point during a stay in Boston. The State House is on the summit of Beacon Hill, and a fifteen- or thirty-minute walk will reveal the riches of the hill. Developed as a residential community in the early nineteenth century, Beacon Hill is characterized by brick townhouses, many with large, purple-paned windows; brightly painted doors with brass knockers; and window boxes vibrant with colorful flowers in the summer. Its handsome streets, such as Mount Vernon and Chestnut, have brick sidewalks, gas lanterns, and carved iron gateways leading to small gardens. The hill's urban gems include Louisburg Square, with its private park, and Acorn Street, a narrow cobblestone lane of handsome townhouses.

"Throughout the years the Hill has been home for many of Boston's most distinguished families, most skilled artists, most talented statesman, most

Shaw—54th Regiment Memorial by Augustus Saint-Gaudens. (Susan VanEtten)

learned scholars, and most astute businessmen, as well as for Bohemians, young-marrieds, and social freaks. Its better-known residents have included such remarkable persons as Daniel Webster, Louis Brandeis, Julia Ward Howe, Edwin Booth, Nathaniel Hawthorne, Louisa May Alcott, John Singer Sargent, Oliver Wendell Holmes, Samuel Eliot Morison, and Henry James, who once described the Hill's Mt. Vernon Street as the 'only respectable street in America.'" (Schofield)

I lived on Beacon Hill for many years. Suburbanites invariably asked, "How can you live right in the middle of *the city* like that?" My reply was that to someone born in New York City, it seemed more like living in a close-knit village than in a city. Townhouses are only three to four stories high. The people are very friendly. I could walk to work. Amenities such as grocery stores, a hardware store, cafés, antique stores, and a pharmacy are close by on Charles Street at the base of the hill. These more than made up for high rents and difficult parking.

The north, or "back," side of the hill was home to many free blacks in the early nineteenth century. African Americans and white residents were very active in the abolitionist movement. Interested visitors can follow the Black

Heritage Trail, which starts at the African Meeting House of 1806, home to the Museum of Afro-American History, off Joy Street. Self-guided walking maps for this trail are available at tourist information sites.

Directly across from the State House on the other side of Beacon Street is the Shaw–54th Regiment Memorial. It is a memorial to the black soldiers from Massachusetts who marched into battle in the Civil War, led by Col. Robert Gould Shaw, only son of a prominent white Boston family. The memorial, a sympathetic portrayal of black soldiers marching to combat, is the work of prominent sculptor Augustus Saint-Gaudens. It took him fourteen years to complete it.

☆ PARK STREET CHURCH ☆

Cross Beacon Street and walk down the hill on Park Street toward the tall white spire of the Park Street Church, on the corner of Park and Tremont streets.

Park Street Church was founded in 1809 by thirty Congregationalist members of the Old South Meeting House, who did not like the growing Unitarian beliefs of the Old South Church. They commissioned Peter Banner to design "the sightliest building in the country," in the style of architect Christopher Wren of London.

The location had been the site of the town granary, where bushels of wheat were stored for poor people in the eighteenth century. Later, the corner at Park and Tremont streets was dubbed "Brimstone Corner." Some say this is because gunpowder—or brimstone—was stored in an underground crypt in the church during the War of 1812. Others say the brimstone refers to the hell-fire-and-damnation sermons delivered by early preachers in the pulpit of the Park Street Church.

Since its early days the church "has always been active in the vanguard of movements for the reform and betterment of mankind as visualized and interpreted by its membership," which has involved evangelical missionary and social work. (Schofield) In 1810 it became the organizing site for the American Board of Commissioners for Foreign Missions; in 1815, for the American Education Society; in 1817, for America's first Sunday School; in 1819, for missionaries to Hawaii; in 1824, for the Prison Reform Society; and in 1826, for the American Temperance Society.

On July 4, 1829, twenty-four-year-old William Lloyd Garrison stood at the church pulpit to deliver his first address decrying the evils of slavery. He shouted, "I will be heard!" Garrison became publisher of the *Liberator* and a leading abolitionist. Two years later, at a children's holiday party at the church, youngsters sang a song that begins, "My country, 'tis of thee"; thus the hymn "America" was born.

Along Tremont Street, one half block from Park Street Church, is the entrance gate to the Granary Burying Ground.

Sometimes called the "Westminster Abbey of America," because of the number of famous Americans buried here, the Granary Burying Ground contains sixteen hundred graves. These include three signers of the Declaration of Independence (John Hancock, Samuel Adams and Robert Treat Paine), eight governors of Massachusetts, five victims of the Boston Massacre, the first mayor of Boston (John Phillips), Benjamin Franklin's parents, Paul Revere, Peter Faneuil, and James Otis. Also buried here are Revolutionary War soldiers and average citizens of Boston who were laid to rest from 1660 up to the early nineteenth century. Among them is the 1690 stone of Mary Goose, believed by many visitors to be the grave of "Mother Goose," despite skeptical claims to the contrary.

The name of the graveyard refers to its location next to Boston's granary, erected in 1737. Entry is through a granite gate, symbolically adorned with "winged globe, downturned torches and flying hourglasses whose time has run out." (Booth) A sharp right past the gate leads to the graves of John Phillips, the first mayor of Boston, and those of the five citizens murdered in the

Park Street Church, 1809. (Author)

Boston Massacre, including Crispus Attucks, the mulatto–Indian sailor who was the first man killed in the massacre. Nearby is the grave of Samuel Adams, the fiery orator whose incendiary speeches played a large role in convincing the colonists to sever their ties with England.

To the left of the entry gate, near the church, is a boulder with a plaque commemorating James Otis, the lawyer whose speech against the Writs of Assistance in 1761 prefigured the many patriot protests against unfair British domination that would follow until independence was achieved.

In the center of the two-acre graveyard is a large cenotaph, engraved "Franklin." It honors Benjamin Franklin's parents, Josiah and Abiah. (Benjamin, fifteenth of his parents' seventeen children, is buried in

Philadelphia, where he spent most of his life.) Continuing counterclockwise around the main path brings into view the headstone of Mary Goose. Farther along is a small memorial stone engraved with these words: "Paul Revere, Born in Boston, January, 1734; died May, 1818." (His famous midnight ride to Lexington occurred in 1775, when Revere was forty-one.) Next to this marker stands Revere's small headstone.

In the left rear corner of the yard is the table tomb of Peter Faneuil, the benefactor who constructed Faneuil Hall with a marketplace on the ground floor and a meeting hall above. On the path back toward Tremont Street stands a tall white pillar honoring John Hancock. It replaces a tombstone that disappeared over a century ago. (Bahne) The height of the pillar befits the status of Hancock, one of the richest men in the Commonwealth, the president of the First Provincial Congress, and the first native-born Governor of the Commonwealth of Massachusetts. Next to the Hancock monument is a stone marked "Frank, Servant to John Hancock, Esq." who died in 1771 at age 38. The absence of a last name may indicate that Frank was a slave buried next to his master, John Hancock.

☆ KING'S CHAPEL ☆

Walk along Tremont Street to School Street, and cross Tremont Street to King's Chapel.

In the 1680s King James II sent to Boston a chaplain, the Reverend Robert Ratcliffe, whose main mission was to establish an Anglican church in Boston, a city that was dominated by dissenting Puritans. The king also sent over a new royal governor, Sir Edmund Andros, to help get the Anglican church built. For two years Andros used his troops to occupy the Old South Church on Sunday mornings to hold Anglican (later called Episcopalian in the states) services. Since no Puritans would sell him land, in 1688 Andros seized by eminent domain what had been Sir Isaac Johnson's vegetable patch to build a wooden church. The despotic Andros was later driven out of Boston by the colonists.

By the 1740s the original wooden structure had become dilapidated, so the town's wealthiest merchant, Peter Faneuil, took up a subscription to build a new stone church over and around the original wooden structure. Granite quarried in Quincy, eight miles to the south, was shipped to Boston. The huge four-foot-thick granite blocks were hauled from the waterfront by teams of eight oxen. The chapel was designed by architect Peter Harrison from Newport, Rhode Island. In 1749 the cornerstone was laid. Angry Puritan Bostonians expressed their displeasure by hurling garbage. When all the granite blocks were in place, the wooden structure was dismantled and literally thrown out the window.

King's Chapel, 1754. (Susan VanEtten)

King's Chapel officially opened amid much royalist pomp in 1754. Over the years British kings lavished gifts on their Anglican beachhead in the colonies; King James II gave an elaborate pulpit; William and Mary sent money, silver, and cushions; Queen Anne sent vestments; and George III sent silver communion pieces. (Schofield)

The church was used mainly by the British establishment—royal governors and officials as well as army and navy officers—and by Bostonians loyal to the king. Over half the pew holders, who were loyalists, left Boston when the British army evacuated the city in 1776. The Reverend Henry Caner, an outspoken loyalist sympathizer who had been minister for thirty years, abandoned the church and departed for Halifax, Nova Scotia, carrying all the church silver and records with him. After the Tories' departure, *King* was taken out of the church's name, briefly, and it was called Stone Chapel.

The interior of the church is elaborate, unlike the plain stone exterior. There are hand-carved Corinthian columns. A wine-glass-shaped pulpit dates to the original wooden church in 1713. High-walled wooden pews helped preserve warmth during cold New England winters. Along the right wall is the canopied governor's pew. Plaques along the walls tell fascinating tales from the lives of parishioners. In a rear gallery one can see—or hear—a large organ, a replica of New England's first organ, installed in 1713.

In 1785 King's Chapel, the first Episcopal (Anglican) church in New England became the first Unitarian church in America when a radical minister, James Freeman, rewrote the prayerbook, omitting any reference to the Trinity and to special prayers for the king and queen. The minister and his flock were denounced as heretics and excommunicated from the Church of England. King's Chapel still has an active congregation. Summoned by Paul Revere's bell, they gather each Sunday to pray together and sing hymns to the accompaniment of organ music.

✦ KING'S CHAPEL BURYING GROUND ✦

Next to King's Chapel, along Tremont Street, is the burying ground, which predates the church.

The earliest burial plot in Boston originated when Sir Isaac Johnson succumbed to the rigors of his new land in 1630. He asked to be buried in his vegetable plot, as did many other Bostonians who followed him. For thirty years Sir Isaac's tomato patch was the only burial ground in the town of Boston. What is now called King's Chapel Burying Ground is the final resting place for nearly the whole first generation of English settlers. (Booth)

Here you will find the graves of John Winthrop, first governor of the Bay Colony; Puritan minister John Cotton; Mary Chilton, reputedly the first woman to step ashore at Plymouth Rock in 1620; and Charles Bulfinch, the architect of the New State House (whose remains were later reburied at Mt. Auburn Cemetery in Cambridge). Here also lie Elizabeth Pain, model for Hester Prynne in Nathaniel Hawthorne's *The Scarlet Letter,* and William Dawes, famous for his own midnight ride to Lexington.

✦ SITE OF THE FIRST PUBLIC SCHOOL ✦

Proceed one half block down School Street on the left side of the street, and keep your eyes on the sidewalk.

The first public school in the country was the Boston Public Latin School, founded in 1635. (Classes were held at the master's house until the first school building was erected in 1645.) At its site on the present-day sidewalk is a colorful mosaic, *City Carpet,* by artist Lilli Ann Killen Rosenberg. Brass letters and Venetian glass spell out the names of the school's famous alumni, including minister Cotton Mather, patriot Samuel Adams, political leader John Hancock, and jack-of-all-trades Benjamin Franklin. The Puritan fathers (and mothers) considered education very important for boys. One year later in 1636 they established Harvard College across the Charles River in Cambridge. Students entering Harvard, many of

Lilli Ann Killen Rosenberg's City Carpet, marking the site of Boston's first public school. (Susan VanEtten)

them from the Latin School, were expected to follow a strict curriculum of grammar, logic, rhetoric, religion, arithmetic, geometry, metaphysics, astronomy, ethics, natural science, ancient history, Greek, and Hebrew. Latin was not studied formally at Harvard, since it was assumed that the student was already proficient in Latin, learned in a grammar school such as Boston Latin. Boston Latin School and Harvard not only trained ministers for cities and towns throughout New England, but also supplied teachers, lawyers, physicians, merchants, and other professionals.

The Boston Latin School, now coeducational, remains one of the best public schools in Boston. Students are accepted only after stiff competitive examinations. Boston Latin School still requires four years of Latin to graduate and still supplies eager students to Harvard.

★ BENJAMIN FRANKLIN'S STATUE ★

Enter the courtyard in front of the Old Boston City Hall through an iron gate. Franklin's statue is on the left.

Boston's first public portrait statue is a tribute to one of its most outstanding native sons, Benjamin Franklin. The eight-foot bronze likeness of Franklin, cast by Richard S. Greenough, was erected in 1856. The sculptor recounted that he found "the left side of the great man's face philosophical and reflective and the right side funny and smiling."

Largely self-taught, Franklin excelled as a printer, writer, editor, inventor, scientist, military officer, politician, and statesman. He is the only American who signed all four of the critical documents in Revolutionary era history: the Declaration of Independence in 1776, the Treaty of Alliance with France in 1778, the treaty of peace with Great Britain in 1783 and the Constitution of the United States in 1789. (Booth)

Franklin was born in Boston in 1706, the fifteenth of his parents' seventeen children. He was born in a modest house at 17 Milk Street, where today a bust of Franklin and a plaque commemorate the event. Ben was baptized

Statue of Benjamin Franklin in front of Old City Hall. (Author)

at the Old South Church. He attended Boston Latin School for only two years before being apprenticed to his brother James, the printer of the *New England Courant.* Ben set type by hand, ran the press, and hawked papers and broadsides, some of which he had written. When his brother was arrested for upsetting some dignitaries with his articles, Ben took over and published the paper. Eventually Ben split from his abusive brother and master. He sailed to Philadelphia in 1723 at age 17. He had bitterly resented the bullying of his brother and later remarked, "his harsh and tyrannical treatment of me was a means of impressing me with the aversion to arbitrary power that has stuck to me thro' my whole life." Although he spent the rest of his life in Philadelphia and Europe, Benjamin Franklin's literary and political roots remained in Boston.

Franklin's statue stands in front of Old City Hall, an ornate building in the French Second Empire style. Built in 1862, it was a hub of activity for Boston pols for over one hundred years, until 1968. The building, one of the first to be conserved historically despite extensive renovations, houses offices and restaurants. Across the courtyard is the Statue of Josiah Quincy, Boston's second mayor, who first built Quincy Market Place, which is so popular today.

✮ OLD CORNER BOOK STORE ✮

Continue down School Street. On the corner of School and Washington streets you will find the Old Corner Book Store, now called the Globe Corner Book Store.

New ideas have flourished at this site since 1634, when Anne Hutchinson and her husband William built a house here. They held religious meetings that challenged the authority of the Puritan ministers. Refusing to tolerate independent thinking, the ministers banished them and their fourteen children to more tolerant Rhode Island in 1638.

After a fire in 1711 destroyed the existing structure, apothecary Thomas Crease build a solid brick building there, with living quarters upstairs under a gambrel roof and a shop downstairs, with bay windows facing the busy intersection. Crease became wealthy selling the remedies of his day—live leeches, crude opium, mandrake, and herbs such as camomile.

The neighborhood became known as "The Cradle of American Journalism." In 1704 the colony's first paper, *The Newsletter,* was published by postmaster John Campbell. The paper was filled with local news and snippets from the British press. James Franklin, briefly abetted by his apprentice brother Ben, in 1721 began publishing the *New England Courant.* Its critical *Silence Do Good Papers* so offended the authorities that James was jailed. Freedom of the press did not exist yet. The *Boston Gazette,* founded in 1719 and housed nearby, after 1768 printed articles critical of the British authorities and written by Samuel Adams, James Otis, John Hancock, and Dr. Joseph

Warren. Ten different bookstores and publishers have used the site since 1828. (Dunwell)

During the mid–nineteenth century, a period described by literary critic Van Wyk Brooks as the "Flowering of New England," the crossing at School and Washington streets became known as "Parnassus Corner," under publisher William D. Ticknor. When Ticknor entered into partnership with his former apprentice James T. "Jamie" Fields to form Ticknor and Fields, their offices became a gathering place for their stable of authors, including Transcendentalists Ralph Waldo Emerson, Henry David Thoreau, and Margaret Fuller. Other authors whom they published included novelist Nathaniel Hawthorne, poet Henry Wadsworth Longfellow, abolitionist Harriet Beecher Stowe, and the popular British authors Charles Dickens and William Thackeray.

The Old Corner Book Store soon became the favorite meeting place for New England authors as well as visitors from abroad. Conversations over claret spawned the Saturday Club. Emerson, Thoreau, and Louisa May Alcott often took the train in from Concord to attend. These meetings led to the publication of the *Atlantic Monthly,* edited by Fields and printed on a press at the rear of the house, literally driven by horsepower, that is, by a team of two Canadian horses "liberally stoked by oats and hay." The *Atlantic Monthly* is still published in Boston today—minus the horses.

✯ OLD SOUTH MEETING HOUSE ✯

Walk across Washington Street, turn right, and walk a half block to the Old South Meeting House.

In 1669 a group of orthodox Puritans had built a simple two-story cedar meetinghouse on land that had belonged to Governor John Winthrop. By 1729 the simple tastes of the early Puritans had evolved to suit the more prosperous parishioners of the day. The fashionable Georgian brick structure that still stands, designed by Joshua Blanchard in the style of London's Christopher Wren, boasts Palladian windows, a tower, a belfry, and a 180-foot steeple. The top tier of the two-tier balcony was for slaves; the most famous one to worship here was Phillis Wheatley, who was taught to read and write by her mistress and became a renowned poet.

In the years leading up to the Revolution, the Old South Meeting House, as the largest place of assembly in Boston (larger than Faneuil Hall in pre-Revolutionary times), served as the seat of meetings to protest the tyrannical measures imposed by the British on the colonists. (See Chapter 1.) News of protest meetings here, sparked by articulate speakers such as James Otis, Samuel Adams, and Dr. Joseph Warren, enraged authorities in faraway London.

In 1768 with James Otis as moderator, Bostonians met in Old South and demanded removal of British naval guns from the Boston Harbor. More protests would follow.

"Later, protests were shouted, loud and long, against the Sugar Act and the high cost of distilling rum, against the Stamp Act and the high cost of feeding British troops, against taxation without representation, against trial without jury by British admiralty courts, against the Townshend Acts and the high cost of drinking tea, and against the perpetrators of the Boston Massacre. It must have seemed to Parliament as though Old South wielded the loudest, most outraged, most clamorous voice in all of North America, which of course it did." (Schofield)

Old South Meeting House. (Author)

In 1770, immediately following the Boston Massacre, thousands of angry colonists marched to the Old South. They demanded that all British troops "guarding" Boston be removed. On December 16, 1773 over five thousand Bostonians jammed into Old South to protest the presence of three English ships laden with unwanted tea in the Boston Harbor. Samuel Adams gave the signal that sparked the series of events known as the Boston Tea Party. A year later, on March 6, 1775, Dr. Joseph Warren delivered an oration marking the fifth anniversary of the Boston Massacre. The meeting house was so full that he was forced to climb a ladder and enter through a window. Throughout his oration, his last before he was killed at Bunker Hill, he was taunted by Redcoats in the audience.

Following the Battle of Bunker Hill in June 1775, and during the months Boston was under siege, British general John Burgoyne exacted revenge against the Old South for the years of seditious protest meetings. He drove out the churchgoers and transformed the Old South into an officers club and a riding rink. He ripped out the pews and used them for firewood. He dumped tons of gravel and dirt on the floor. He erected crossbars so the Queen's Light Dragoons could use them for jumping practice. The riders were spurred on by drunken officers and their wives and mistresses, who imbibed rum from the bar they had installed in the upper gallery.

When George Washington drove the British out of Boston in March 1776, one of his first visits was to the Old South. He surveyed the mess and ordered the church restored to the way it was before Redcoats and horses took over. The congregation restored the interior to its former state, including wooden pews, a tall pulpit and candlelight chandeliers.

The Old South survived the devastating Great Fire of 1872, which burned most of the other buildings in the neighborhood. The congregation then sold the building for the paltry sum of $1,350 and moved to a new site in Boston's Back Bay. The Old South Meeting House was on the verge of demolition, but fundraising efforts in 1876, led by a group of prominent Bostonians, raised enough money to purchase the building and its land. This was the first successful effort at historic preservation made in New England. In 1877, the Old South Meeting House was incorporated as a history museum and historic site.

In the 1920s, during a free speech controversy, the Old South Association, in keeping with its long tradition of free public discourse, voted to allow public discussion "without regard to the popularity of any cause." The church opened its doors to controversial speakers denied a platform elsewhere. Today the Old South has an active agenda of public meetings, lectures, concerts, plays, and church services. Visitors today will find exhibits on the building's rich history, as well as a new permanent exhibit called "Voices of Protest."

★ OLD STATE HOUSE ★

After exiting Old South, turn right on Washington Street and follow the trail for two blocks.

Although today it is dwarfed by glass-faced skyscrapers, the Old State House clearly evokes the eighteenth century. Its white cupola surmounts a carved British lion and a unicorn, atop a brick building of two and a half stories. Here British royal governors fought, often unsuccessfully, to impose their will on colonial assemblies at this early seat of both royal and colonial power.

The first Town House, as it was called, at this site was erected in 1658 at the busy intersection of King Street, which led to the Long Wharf, and Road to the Neck, today's State and Washington Streets. It was paid for by a bequest from Captain Robert Keayne, a wealthy tailor who founded and was first captain of the Ancient and Honorable Artillery Company. Keayne had been denounced by the Puritans for "making too much profit" and had been forced to confess publicly his "covetous and corrupt heart." (Booth) In his will, which ran for fifty-four pages, he left the town three hundred pounds to erect a wooden Town House that would include a marketplace with shelter for "the country people that come with their provisions" as well as rooms for the legislature and for a library, and an armory for the Ancient and Honorable Artillery Company, of which he was a member.

"For the next 53 years the Town House was at the center of a number of crises and dramatic events. It was the working headquarters for the Royal

Governors, the Governor's Council, the representatives to the General Court [legislature], the judiciary and the leading town officials. Its walls echoed with exciting trials of pirates captured at sea, the clanging of weaponry as King Philip's Indian warriors burned their way towards Boston in 1675, the outcries for and against sending the pirate Captain Kidd back to England for a London gallows, the uproar over the expulsion of Governor Sir Edmond Andros." (Schofield)

In 1711 a raging fire burned the Town House to the ground. In 1713 the town built a larger Town House, which stood until 1747, when another fire totally destroyed the interior of the building, all the books and records within, and portraits of the king and queen. Only the bare brick walls were left standing. The Town House was rebuilt in 1750. The interior features a staircase leading to the second floor, "seat of the Vice-Regal State of the Governors under the Crown," a small court chamber, and a middle room for members of the Massachusetts Assembly, described as "twenty eight of the most prominent friends of the King." (Linden)

It was in the Town House in 1760 that colonists heard about the coronation of George III. In 1761 James Otis delivered a fiery four-hour speech here to the Crown's representatives, opposing the Writs of Assistance—entry permits that allowed royal customs officials to break down any colonial door, presumably looking for illegal hidden contraband. The colonists detested the despotism implied by these arbitrary searches and vigorously supported Otis's protests. John Adams, describing the historical significance of Otis's speech some fifty years later, stated, "Then and there the child Independence was born."

Heady arguments between royal officials and colonial representatives followed the Sugar Act of 1764, the Stamp Act of 1765, and the Townshend Acts of 1767. Because of mob protests and import boycotts, the Crown dispatched four regiments of Redcoats to Boston in

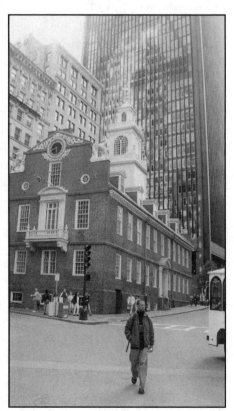

Old State House, 1713. (Author)

1768, two from Halifax and two from Ireland. Incidents between patrolling and parading soldiers and taunting Bostonians increased as the months went by and provided the perfect setting for trouble. And trouble came, big time. On March 5, 1770, young men throwing snowballs at British guards provoked a fusillade, killing five Bostonians, an event henceforth known to the world as the Boston Massacre. Today a ring of cobblestones on a traffic island on the east side of the Old State House marks the actual site of the Boston Massacre.

After the British evacuated Boston on March 17, 1776, the Town House again became the seat of the Massachusetts legislature, which had been meeting in the countryside since 1774. The first public reading of the Declaration of Independence, delivered to an excited crowd below the east balcony, took place on July 18, 1776. That night the celebration included tearing down and burning all British emblems, including the lion and the unicorn. (It was another hundred years before they were restored.) Today on every July 4 the Declaration is read again from the east balcony.

John Hancock, in his best red velvet coat and blue satin waistcoat, was inaugurated there in 1780 as the first elected governor of the Commonwealth of Massachusetts. In 1783 the Treaty of Paris, ending the Revolution, was read from the balcony. And in 1789 George Washington stood on a platform at the west end of the building to review an honorary procession of soldiers and tradesmen. Finally, in 1798 the governor led a long procession of Commonwealth officials from the Old State House up Beacon Hill to take possession of the golden-domed New State House.

The Old State House fell on hard times during the next hundred years. It was occupied by a hodgepodge of commercial establishments, including cobblers, wig makers, and wine merchants. It served briefly as the City Hall from 1830 to 1844, after which time the tradespeople returned. It became so run down that it appeared certain to be razed. Then came an offer from the City of Chicago to move it, brick by brick, to the shore of Lake Michigan "for all America to revere." That did it. Shame-faced Bostonians banded together to restore the building. They formed the Bostonian Society to preserve it, which today opens the Old State House to visitors who can enjoy displays about its rich history.

☆ FANEUIL HALL ☆

From the Old State House, continue on the trail across State and Congress Streets. Follow the trail down Congress Street to Faneuil Hall. As you approach Faneuil Hall, stop to admire the statue of Samuel Adams by Anne Whitney.

Nicknamed the "Cradle of Liberty," Faneuil Hall witnessed much fiery patriotic oratory against the British in pre-Revolutionary times. It is still used frequently for community meetings.

Peter Faneuil, according to John Hancock, was "the topmost merchant in all the town" of Boston, due to his successes in foreign trade and shipping. His family had fled France in 1685 along with a million other Huguenots to escape the harsh anti-Protestant restrictions of King Louis XIV. Peter's Uncle Andrew became extremely wealthy as a merchant in Boston. He promised to leave all his money to his nephew only if Peter never married. The younger man agreed. So Peter, "a fat, squat, lame man, hip-short with a high shoe," became known as "the jolly bachelor." His late-night parties were consistent with this reputation. He even named one of his ships the *Jolly Bachelor.* When Uncle Andrew died in 1738, Peter, forever single, came into all his money.

Peter decided that the town needed a central marketplace where merchants and customers could accomplish all sorts of transactions within a convenient area. The location: Dock Square on the waterfront. He proposed to build at his own expense "a noble and complete structure to be improved for a market for the sole use, benefit and advantage of the town." The market was completed in 1742. Its stalls and exchange booths faced out on all four sides. Peter had directed that a second story town meeting hall be added above the marketplace. Thus, then and now, commerce took place downstairs and politics upstairs. Grateful Bostonians decided to name the building for him: Faneuil Hall. Sadly, the first use of the public meeting hall was a memorial service for Peter Faneuil after his death in March 1743.

Faneuil Hall rapidly became Boston's center of commerce and politics. When it was destroyed by fire in 1761, it was rapidly rebuilt and enlarged. In 1805 the building was widened, and a third story was added by architect Charles Bulfinch.

From the day of its opening, Faneuil Hall became the place to go for anybody interested in hearing the raw opinions of orators and patriots. Many of the stirring and emotional events connected with the rebellion against the Crown had their origins here. John Hancock and Sam Adams frequently used the Faneuil Hall rostrum to cry out against British oppression. Here the Stamp Act was denounced, and its repeal celebrated. Here on November 5, 1773, patriots held the first of their several Tea Party rallies. (Schofield)

Samuel Adams was described by his arch enemy Governor Hutchinson as "The Man of the Town Meeting . . . here he animated, enlightened, fortified, and roused the admiring throng; he seemed to gather them together . . . as a hen gathereth her chickens under her wings." (Bahne)

During the siege of Boston in 1775, occupying British troops used the hall as a barracks and theater. George Washington, as first President, was honored here at an enormous banquet in 1789.

The cupola of Faneuil Hall has been topped by a famous gilded grasshopper weathervane since 1742. Why a grasshopper? No one knows for sure. The grasshopper disappeared mysteriously in 1973 and was recovered just as mys-

Quincy Market, 1826. (Author)

teriously after a steeplejack convicted of drug charges offered a tip. It was found under some old flags in the cupola.

After the Revolution, Faneuil Hall continued its tradition of providing an open forum for ideas as it hosted debates by abolitionists, advocates of temperance and women's rights, politicians of every shade, and pro- and anti-war advocates stretching from the War of 1812 to the Vietnam War. I remember the evening when my wife proudly received her citizenship papers here in a large naturalization ceremony for new citizens from many lands. I also remember well-attended book readings by famous authors, such as John Updike.

National Park Service rangers present historical talks at Faneuil Hall every half hour, from 9:00 A.M. to 5:00 P.M. seven days a week. When visiting the Assembly Hall, note the huge painting hanging over the stage in the front. It shows Daniel Webster speaking before the U.S. Senate. It was originally commissioned by King Louis-Philippe of France in 1842, but by the time it was finished seven years later the king had been deposed; thus the painting hangs in Boston, not at Versailles.

Upstairs over the hall is the Armory Museum of the Ancient and Honorable Artillery Company. The "Ancients," as they are called, date back to 1637, when they were formed to protect the town from Indian attack. Although they seldom fought as a unit, individual members of the company, America's first and oldest militia, have fought in every American conflict since the seventeenth century.

★ Faneuil Hall Marketplace (Quincy Market) ★

Faneuil Hall Marketplace is but a few steps east of Faneuil Hall.

Today Faneuil Hall Marketplace, also called by its original name, Quincy Market, is one of the most popular tourist attractions in America. Its combination of shops, restaurants, and performers in the ambiance of a tastefully preserved 180-year-old marketplace is an all-season draw for both tourists and Bostonians.

Originally designed by Alexander Parrish in 1826, when Josiah Quincy was mayor of Boston, the central granite marketplace building was constructed in the Greek Revival style with columned porticos at either end and a central domed pavilion. It was designed to supplement the ground floor markets in Faneuil Hall. The 535-foot-long central building housed scores of butchers and grocers. By the 1960s it had fallen into a state of neglect and disrepair. Redevelopment by James Rouse and architect Benjamin Thompson, which was completed in 1976, restored the central marketplace building and the flanking North Market and South Market buildings to their former role as attractive destinations for shoppers and diners. The successful restoration has inspired other American cities to revive their downtown areas.

Follow the Freedom Trail from Faneuil Hall to the North End to Paul Revere's house at 19 North Square.

On the way, you'll pass the New England Holocaust Memorial, not officially a stop on the Freedom Trail but one of Boston's newest and most distinctive landmarks. This monument offers a unique opportunity for reflection on the true meaning of freedom and oppression and on the importance of society's respect for human rights. The memorial features six luminous glass towers set on a black granite path and etched with six million numbers commemorating the Jewish lives destroyed by the Holocaust. Each tower, representing the chimney of a Nazi death camp, is set over a smoldering chamber bearing the name of one of these camps. Visitors walk thorough the towers and confront information about both the victims and the heroes of the Holocaust.

Completed in 1995, the memorial moved Elie Wiesel, Holocaust survivor and Nobel Prize winning author, to say: "Look at these towers, passerby, and try to imagine what they really mean, what they symbolize what they evoke. . . . We must look for hope—as a great Hasidic master said, 'If you look for a spark, you will find it in the ashes.'"

★ Paul Revere House ★

Paul Revere was a man of huge accomplishments. He became a legend thanks to Longfellow's 1861 narrative poem, " Paul Revere's Ride." The house where he lived with his family from 1770 to 1800 serendipitously still stands, the only wooden seventeenth-century house in Boston. It is now called the Paul Revere House.

Revere stood out in many fields: as a metal smith working in gold, silver, and copper; an engraver of patriotic broadsides and of currency; a soldier; a patriotic express rider; an organizer for the Sons of Liberty; and later in his life an operator of foundries for bells and cannons and a copper-rolling mill. His success in organizing for the patriotic cause was enhanced by his ability to move easily among all strata of Boston society, as a Mason, a member of artisan and religious groups, a Whig leader. and a participant in many political clubs. (Fischer)

The parsonage of Increase Mather, the Puritan minister of the first North Church in Boston and father of Cotton Mather, originally stood at the site, but was destroyed in the Great Fire of 1676. It was rebuilt in 1680 as a two-story clapboard house with a second-story overhang. Its windows have diamond-shaped leaded panes. In 1770 Revere moved in with his first wife, Sara Orne, and their eight children. Three years later upon Sara's death Revere remarried. His second wife, Rachel Walker, bore him eight more children, only five of whom survived past childhood. Paul Revere was truly prolific, in family life as in work.

✶ OLD NORTH CHURCH ✶

Continue left on North Street, following the Freedom Trail. Take first left onto Prince Street and right onto Hanover Street. Walk two blocks, then cross Hanover Street into Paul Revere Mall, with the Statue of Paul Revere by sculptor Cyrus Dallin. Then walk to Old North Church at 193 Salem Street.

The Old North Church, Boston's oldest, is probably also the best-known church in Boston due to its role in Longfellow's legend-making poem about Paul Revere's ride. On April 18, 1775, Revere's friend, sexton Robert Newman, hung two lanterns atop the steeple to signal that British troops were departing by boat across the river, not by land over the Boston Neck to march to Lexington and Concord. (Today one of the two original lanterns is displayed in the Concord Museum.) Revere was then rowed to Charlestown, where waiting patriots who had seen the signal gave him a horse to begin his famous midnight ride to alert the countryside west of Boston that the British Regulars were out.

The church, also called Christ Church, was built in 1723 as the second Anglican church in Boston. (King's Chapel was the first.) It is in the style of Sir Christopher Wren's London churches, with a tall 190-foot steeple. The steeple has since been rebuilt many times in the wake of gales and hurricanes. The Church has an eight-bell carillon, brought from England in 1744. A

Paul Revere House, 1680. (Susan VanEtten)

young Paul Revere was one of the church's early bell ringers. The chimes are still rung regularly after Sunday morning services. Brass plates on the wooden pews still carry the names of Revolutionary era parishioners, some of whose descendants still worship here. Underground crypts house the bones of some of their ancestors. They had to be church members, of course, to be buried under the Old North Church.

★ COPP'S HILL BURYING GROUND ★

Cross Salem Street and follow the trail up Hull Street to Copp's Hill Burying Ground.

Copp's Hill has always been the North End's highest piece of land. Briefly it was known as Windmill Hill, since the early Puritans set up windmills here to catch the ocean breezes. Starting in 1660 it was used as a burying ground. Near the Charter Street gate of Copp's Hill Burying Ground is the tomb of the Mathers, father Increase and son Cotton, powerful Puritan ministers of the late seventeenth and early eighteenth centuries. Cotton Mather's 1689 book *Memorable Providences Relating to Witchcraft and Possessions* helped set the stage for the witchcraft hysteria in Salem. Robert Newman, the sexton who hung the lanterns in Old North Church, is interred in tomb number 27 along the Snow Hill Street fence.

Monument to Prince Hall in Copp's Hill Burying Ground. (Author)

Nearby is a tall black marble obelisk, a monument to Prince Hall, leader of Boston's early free black community. Originally a slave from Medford, he won his freedom by enlisting and fighting in the Continental Army. After the Revolution he settled in a section of the North End at the foot of Copp's Hill, popular with free blacks. It was called "New Guinea" and over one thousand of its residents are buried at Copp's Hill. Hall became a leader of the free blacks and established the first black Masonic lodge as well as a school for black children.

During the Revolution, British troops placed their artillery on Copp's Hill to guard Boston Harbor from French ships. In June 1775 their six cannons bombarded Charlestown, burning the town to the ground during the Battle of Bunker Hill. British generals John Burgoyne and Henry Clinton used Copp's Hill as a command post during the battle, where they witnessed the fire and slaughter across the water. British Regulars later used tombstones here for target practice. Their bullet holes are still visible for all to see.

☆ USS *CONSTITUTION*—"OLD IRONSIDES" ☆

By foot, continue on the Freedom Trail down Hull Street, over the North Washington Street Bridge to the Charlestown Navy Yard. It is also possible to go the Charlestown by subway from the Haymarket stop, by bus, by water shuttle from the Long Wharf, by tourist trolley, or by car.

USS *Constitution*, "Old Ironsides," never experienced naval defeat, only victory, from the time it was launched in 1797. Currently it is the oldest commissioned ship in the world. Its crew is on active duty with the navy, and its permanent home port is Boston.

George Washington commissioned *Constitution* and five other frigates to "provide a naval armament" to protect freedom of the high seas for the fledging nation. *Constitution* was built at Edmund Hartt's shipyard at the foot of Copp's Hill across the water from where it is now berthed. It cost $302,718. The ship is 204 feet long, with a 43-foot beam, and made of white oak from Massachusetts and Maine, as well as live oak and yellow pine from Georgia and South Carolina. It could sail at 13.5 knots with a crew of 450 men and armed with forty-four (later fifty-two) guns.

Constitution's string of uninterrupted victories is the pride of U.S. naval history. In 1798 it fought French privateers along the East Coast and in the West Indies in the undeclared war threatening America's commerce. From 1803 to 1805 it fought in the Mediterranean against the Barbary pirates and Tripoli (hence "to the shores of Tripoli" in the "Marine Hymn"). In the War of 1812 *Constitution* faced the formidable British navy off the coast of New Jersey. It earned the nickname "Old Ironsides" after withstanding cannon fire from the H.M.S. *Guerriere* off the coast of Nova Scotia. The British captain declared, "Huzzah, her sides are made of iron," as the British cannonballs appeared to bounce off the thick wooden hull of *Constitution.* The American frigate bore down on its adversary and, in less than half an hour of cannon broadsides, pounded *Guerriere* to splinters.

"Old Ironsides" triumphed again off the coast of Brazil, subduing the forty-seven-gun *Java.* Two years later in a one-against-two clash off the coast of Portugal, the vessel fought and won against the corvette *Cyane* and the sloop *Levant.* This victory helped America win the War of 1812, which concluded with the Treaty of Ghent in 1814, again confirming American independence in the face of British aggression. *Constitution* fought in over forty engagements and never lost a fight. (Linden, Schofield)

USS Constitution, "Old Ironsides," at the Charlestown Navy Yard. (Susan VanEtten)

Constitution withstood several serious demolition threats over the past two centuries. First, in 1830, a rousing poem by physician Oliver Wendell Holmes saved the ship for further service. Retired after the Civil War, *Constitution* was used as a training ship. A restoration in 1925 was financed partially by pennies saved by children throughout the country. The ship underwent another major renovation in time for its bicentennial in 1997.

The ship stays in its berth at the Charlestown Navy Yard all year except for an annual turnaround ceremony around the Boston Harbor each July 4. Following September 11, 2001, the US Navy severely restricted visitation aboard *Constitution*. While limited public tours were available at this writing, visitors are advised to consult the tour schedule.

USS *Constitution* Museum houses exhibits, a theater, historical artifacts, and interactive displays, which bring alive the dramatic adventures of the ship. It is located in Building 22 behind the ship's berth.

USS *Cassin Young* is a destroyer that was on active duty from 1943, when she saw action in the Pacific, to 1960. Berthed on the other side of the dock from *Constitution,* she represents the fourteen similar American ships built at the Boston Navy Yard during World War II, although she herself was built in California.

★ Bunker Hill Monument ★

Follow the Freedom Trail out of the navy yard and proceed to Adams Street toward Monument Square to the Bunker Hill Monument.

The cataclysmic Battle of Bunker Hill on June 17, 1775—the crucial first formal battle of the American Revolution—is described in detail in Chapter 4. This monument commemorates that historic conflict. Its cornerstone was laid by Marquis de Lafayette on the fiftieth anniversary of the battle.

The Bunker Hill Monument Association built the monument between 1825 and 1842 with stops and starts due to monetary problems. Money to finish the monument was raised from fairs held by the "mothers and daughters of Boston" and through generous benefactors such as Amos Lawrence, Sarah Hale, and Judah Touro of New Orleans. Designed by architect Solomon Willard and based on the Egyptian Revival style, the memorial consists of a memorial granite obelisk that stands 221 feet tall. America's first commercial railway was constructed in Quincy, Massachusetts, to haul quarried granite blocks to an ocean dock for shipment to Charlestown.

The lodge at the base of the monument contains a small museum with a diorama of the battle. National Park Service rangers are available to narrate interesting facts about the battle. The observatory is on top of the shaft. The ascent to the top requires 294 steps (sorry, no elevator). Visitors should be in good shape to attempt the climb, but the view from the top is outstanding.

Musket-firing demonstrations are also offered Fridays through Sundays during the summer.

The Bunker Hill Pavilion (which serves as the Charlestown Navy Yard Visitors Center) on Constitution Road close to USS *Constitution* shows a multimedia reenactment called "The Whites of Their Eyes," which portrays the Battle of Bunker Hill as seen through the eyes of the combatants.

★ SOURCES ★

Bahne, Charles. *Complete Guide to Boston's Freedom Trail.* Newtowne Publishing, 1993.

Booth, Robert. *Boston's Freedom Trail.* Globe Pequot Press, 1994.

Boston National Historical Park. *Boston and the American Revolution; Bunker Hill; Freedom Trail* (map). Charlestown Navy Yard, Boston National Historical Park, 1998.

Fleming, Thomas. *Liberty! The American Revolution.* Viking, 1997.

Freedom Trail Foundation. *Boston's Freedom Trail: Map and Guide.* Freedom Trail Foundation, 2000.

Ketcham, Richard (ed.) *The American Heritage Book of the American Revolution.* Simon & Schuster, 1958.

Linden, Blanche. *Boston's Freedom Trail.* Back Bay Press, 1996.

Schofield, William. *Freedom by the Bay: Boston Freedom Trail.* Rand McNally, 1974.

Whitehill, Walter M. *Boston: A Topographical History.* Harvard University, 1968.

Colonial Idioms
Alive Today

☆ ☆ ☆ ☆ ☆ ☆ ☆ ☆ ☆ ☆ ☆ ☆ ☆ ☆

Flash in the pan. . . . At loggerheads . . . Read the riot act . . . A windfall.

Colorful idioms all, and what they share in common is a modern usage connected to an eighteenth-century past. Although today's usage may differ somewhat, these terms and others like them might have been heard in Concord in 1775. Come discover the fascinating origins of some peculiar phrases.

When colonial gunsmith Joshia Meriam constructed a musket, it was usually accomplished and paid for in three parts—lock (firing mechanism), stock (wood), and barrel (metal tube). Once completed, the item as a whole was given to its purchaser. Today when one obtains an item complete with all its parts, one obtains it "lock, stock and barrel."

If militiaman Thaddeus Blood placed his musket in the safety position (half-cocked) when he entered battle, he had to remember to advance to full-cock or the weapon would not fire, and he would be in trouble. A person "going off half-cocked" is not successful due to lack of preparation and forethought.

Nathan Stowe might prime his musket (putting a small measure of powder in the pan), load the main charge to the barrel, and fire, only to see the priming powder explode. This was known as a "flash in the pan," or a misfire. Today the term means a sudden brief success not likely to be repeated or followed by a greater success. Perhaps Stowe needed a new flint but couldn't afford or was unwilling to pay for such. He might take a knife and chip, or skin, pieces from the old flint until it was serviceable. Today, a cheap or thrifty person is called a "skinflint."

Other idioms may be traced to eighteenth-century taverns. As a reminder, Thomas Munroe, tavern keeper, might use chalk to mark upon his wall the bill of a patron who wished to pay at a later time. Today, when something is "chalked up" to experience, it is a possibly unfortunate happening taken as a lesson—with an account mark made in the memory. Also, people who quarrel or enter a confrontation are said to be "at loggerheads." Colonial tavern keeper Amos Wright used a heated loggerhead (a long metal bar with a ball on the end) to warm drinks. Patrons sometimes used them in fights.

Grog was a cheap eighteenth-century drink of rum and water invented by a ship's captain to water down sailors' daily liquor rations in hopes of ending drunken brawls. Today one who consumes too much alcohol may appear "groggy," or mildly intoxicated. Keeper Ephraim Jones might yell to rowdy patrons to "mind their p's and q's" (pints and quarts of drink), and today the term still refers to watching one's manners and conduct—behaving properly.

If we receive unexpected good fortune (usually money) it is called "a windfall." For Jonas Bateman in the 1770s, it would have meant that trees or limbs had been blown down by wind and could easily be obtained for firewood. The term had another specific meaning as well. The king's agents marked certain trees for shipbuilding use by the Royal Navy. Tampering with them brought severe punishment. But if a storm blew such a tree down, it could be claimed by anyone—a windfall.

Have you ever been "read the riot act," or been informed in an angry manner that your conduct was wrong and must stop? The Riot Act of 1715 was meant to address groups whose gathering threatened the peace. A magistrate could read part of the act, commanding people to disperse in the king's name or face punitive action. In the 1880s Americans began using the term to mean "scold."

Purchase Brown, a farmer during the 1770s, would "earmark" his animals with a distinctive brand to denote ownership or purpose.

Citizens would gather annually on muster day to watch the militia drill, enjoy food and drink, socialize, and have a fun time. They had a "field day."

When John Buttrick, Jr., retired for the night, he probably would sleep on bedding of straw. In today's usage he would "hit the hay." Melicent Barrett might tighten the rope supports strung between the wooden sides of her bed frame (no metal springs existed then) to ensure a good night's sleep. She would then "sleep tight."

By reading this chapter, you took "pot luck" — accepting what was available, while not sure what you might receive. Had you visited a home or tavern 225 years ago, and the owner had not had the chance to prepare a proper meal, you would have eaten whatever was in the oven pot—taken a chance—taken pot luck.

—D. Michael Ryan

☆ SOURCES ☆

Kirkpatrick, E. M., and C. M. Schwarz. *The Wordsworth Dictionary of Idioms.* 1995.
Lederer, Richard M., Jr. *Colonial American English.* 1985.

Towns of the
Battle Road
and Beyond

George Washington assuming command of the Continental Army on Cambridge Common, July 3, 1775. (Cambridge Historical Society)

Cambridge: Puritans, Patriots, Tories, and Scholars

★ ★ ★ ★ ★ ★ ★ ★ ★ ★ ★ ★ ★ ★ ★ ★ ★

C ambridge's roles in the American Revolution were as varied as the lives of the people who lived there in the 1770s. Over 90 percent of the town's approximately two thousand residents were descendants of the seven hundred Puritans who had sailed from England in 1630. They had settled on the north bank of the Charles River, eight miles upstream from Boston. Their dream was to build a community that was purer and closer to the Bible than those they left behind in England.

In Newtowne (renamed Cambridge in 1638, after England's university town) they laid out an orderly grid of streets that ran down to the river. Each family owned a modest house in the village, farmed their planting fields on the outskirts of town, and shared common land for grazing livestock. Basically the Puritans re-created the pattern of the English villages they had left behind, as was the case in most other New England towns. Shortly thereafter they built a meetinghouse (church), a school, and a marketplace.

In 1636 they founded the first college in North America, in order to train young men for the Puritan ministry and teach them how to be godly citizens. They named it in honor of the Charlestown minister, John Harvard, who donated his library of several hundred books and half his estate to the college.

By the 1770s descendants of these original Puritan farmers and clergymen were farmers, artisans (blacksmiths, carpenters, shoemakers, tailors, coopers, saddlers), and merchants; a few were owners of new businesses such as law practices, distilleries, and countinghouses. These men had few outside economic resources; they relied completely on the local economy. As crises about taxes and political control escalated in the 1770s, by and large these men opposed the Crown. They supported local interests and called for more local autonomy from London. Lacking meaningful ties to King George III or his royal representatives in Massachusetts, they became patriots. They were willing to sacrifice a secure but subservient future for the promise of more political, social, and

Paul Revere engraving of Harvard College in the eighteenth century. (American Antiquarian Society)

economic freedom, which they hoped independence from Britain would bring. (Bunting)

A smaller group of wealthy families who settled in large country estates in Cambridge could be described as loyalist, oligarchic, and Anglican. They either were descended from the few Puritan families, like the Brattles and the Foxcrofts, who had acquired wealth and subsequently lost their Puritan ways, or, like the Phipses and the Vassalls, had substantial income that originated from outside of Cambridge. They prospered on income from plantations in the West Indies, from profitable mercantile businesses in Boston, or from payments for services rendered to the king. Cambridge loyalists worshipped at their own Anglican church, Christ Church. They gave lavish parties, planted lush gardens in lieu of farming, socialized mostly with one another and frequently intermarried. Most of these few elite families clustered in spacious mansions with extensive grounds on the Watertown Road in the west end of Cambridge, later named Brattle Street, then as now also called "Tory Row." (Bunting) Several other Tory families lived on huge estates on the eastern shore of Fresh Pond. (Krim)

These Cambridge Tories led the good life, but not for long. By accepting royal favors, supporting the Crown, and rejecting the rebels, they hoped to keep their special privileges and maintain the aristocratic status quo. Unfortunately for them, when the Revolution started after the Battles of Lexington and Concord and after the Battle of Bunker Hill in 1775, the provisional government expropriated and later confiscated most Tory estates.

The newly homeless loyalists were forced to flee, many of them departing with the British fleet when it evacuated from Boston. They headed first for

Halifax, Nova Scotia, where many remained. The rest sailed for England where they settled permanently.

Ironically, the loyalists' luxurious houses were used as barracks for citizen-soldiers who gathered from rustic country towns. They joined the fledgling Continental Army, then encamped in Cambridge. The Vassall mansion on Brattle Street (today called Longfellow House) became General George Washington's headquarters during the siege of Boston in 1775–1776.

Cambridge's first direct contact with the coming conflict occurred late in the evening of April 18 and early on the morning of April 19, 1775. William Dawes galloped over Boston Neck, through Roxbury, and along Cambridge's Great Road (today's Massachusetts Avenue) to alert the countryside that British troops were advancing to Concord to seize hidden weapons. Several hours later, seven hundred British Regulars under Lieutenant Colonel Francis Smith were ferried across the Charles River to land below the Phips farm at Lechmere's Point in East Cambridge. After a delay in the swampy landing spot, at about 2:00 A.M. Smith finally led his men westward from Cambridge along the Great Road toward Lexington, then Concord.

British general Thomas Gage had ordered a second expedition of about one thousand fresh troops under Brigadier General Hugh Percy to be sent from Boston toward Concord to relieve Smith's exhausted and depleted Regulars. This relief force did not leave Boston until after daybreak (after the clashes between Smith's Redcoats and colonial militia and Minute Men at Lexington Green and Concord's North Bridge had both finished). Percy's troops marched over the land route via Roxbury. They were delayed further due to sabotage to the Great Bridge done by local patriots and did not reach Cambridge until midmorning. They did not rendezvous with Colonel Smith's exhausted, retreating soldiers in Lexington until about 3:00 P.M. (Krim)

The combined British forces of Smith and Percy, now totaling about seventeen hundred men, "had little choice but to return along the Great Road (through Menotomy—today's Arlington—and Cambridge). The road was bristling with Minute Men and militia awaiting an opportunity to harass the Redcoats." (Krim) Trying to avoid certain ambush in Cambridge, Percy led his regiment to the left fork, the road to Charlestown.

Percy's flankers discovered three rebels crouching behind dry casks in Jacob Watson's yard. The Redcoats killed all three: Major Isaac Gardner, John Hicks, and Moses Richardson. Gardner was the most senior of the colonials killed on April 19 and the first Harvard graduate (class of 1747) to die for the cause of liberty. For good measure, the British also killed William Marcy, a simple-minded bystander, who had turned out to watch a parade. Fourteen-year-old Edward Barber of Charlestown was shot in the window of his house.

Percy, using his cannons, shelled the militiamen massed farther down the Cambridge Road and, "under the cover of his fire, the column marched past the danger point and on towards Charlestown." When they staggered over the Charlestown Neck and climbed up to the safety of Bunker Hill, it was past 7:00 P.M. and dark. From Charlestown the exhausted British soldiers, many wounded, were ferried back to Boston by Royal Navy longboats. (Galvin)

On June 14, 1775, eight weeks after the incidents at Lexington and Concord and three days before the Battle of Bunker Hill, the Continental Congress in Philadelphia elected Virginia's militia colonel George Washington as commander in chief. He was to replace Massachusetts general Artemis Ward as commander of the disjointed bands of New England militia surrounding Boston, now to be called the Continental Army. John Adams, seconded by his cousin Samuel Adams, had proposed Washington, much to the chagrin of their fellow Massachusetts delegate, the presiding official John Hancock, who had coveted the commanding general appointment for himself. (Fleming)

Washington arrived in Cambridge on July 3. It is doubtful that he assumed command and surveyed nine thousand assembled militiamen in an elaborate ceremony under the spreading elm on the Cambridge Common, as local legend has it. This famous scene, never substantiated, was depicted in many subsequent illustrations and added mythical stature to the already impressive reality of the modest yet ambitious farmer-soldier-statesman who was George Washington. (Batchelder, Rees)

What Washington did find in Cambridge was, in his words, "a mixed multitude of people . . . under very little discipline, order, or government." (Ketchum) The disparate men who were to form his new army lacked training. They were short of tents, blankets, sanitary facilities, muskets, powder, ammunition, and bayonets. They did not firmly commit to fixed terms of enlistment because of their other responsibilities or their whim of the moment, so their availability was tenuous. For the intriguing story of how Washington molded undisciplined mobs of men into an effective fighting force, I commend you to authors such as Washington, Ketchum, and Fleming. It is worth gaining deeper insight into the colonists' unlikely ultimate victory against the British. And it all began in Cambridge.

★ REVOLUTIONARY WAR SITES TO VISIT TODAY IN CAMBRIDGE ★

The **Cambridge Common** (1631), a triangular park between Massachusetts Avenue, Garden Street, and Waterhouse Street, has been the focal point for Cambridge's economic, social, religious, and political life for over 350 years. According to legend, on July 3, 1775, under a spreading elm George Washington took command of nine thousand men who were to form the newly created Continental Army. A plaque on the Garden Street side of the Common commemorates the event most historians believe is more myth than reality. During the siege of Boston of 1775–1776, the Common served

Old Burying Ground and Christ Church, 1761. (Cambridge Historical Commission)

as the main campground for the tents of General Washington's army. Plaques on the entry gateways celebrate Washington's stay in Cambridge.

The **Cambridge Burying Ground** (1635) is situated between the First Parish Church and Christ Church on Garden Street. The slate headstones illustrate changing fashions in tombstone sculpture, ranging from medieval-style death's- heads of the late seventeenth century to Renaissance-inspired winged cherubs of the eighteenth century to Neoclassical urn-and-willow mourning motifs of the early nineteenth century. "From realistic to symbolic, they thus chronicle changing attitudes towards death." (Bunting)

Christ Church (1761), on Garden Street, designed by architect Peter Harrison, is the oldest church in Cambridge. Its congregants were wealthy Anglican loyalists. When its Tory members departed from Cambridge in 1775, Connecticut militia used the church as their barracks. They melted the organ pipes for bullets. George and Martha Washington worshipped here during their stay in Cambridge.

Harvard University (1636) still includes early buildings that were standing when William Dawes galloped over the nearby Great Road (Massachusetts Avenue) toward Lexington, sounding an alarm to the countryside on April 18, 1775. British troops advancing to Concord marched by Harvard on the same route.

Wadsworth House (1727), at 1341 Massachusetts Avenue and Harvard Square, was built as the official residence of Harvard presidents and served this purpose for nine presidents until 1849. When George Washington first arrived in Cambridge in 1775, it served briefly as his house and headquarters.

A walk around **Harvard Yard**, off Harvard Square, takes the visitor past some of Harvard's most historic buildings. The oldest Harvard building extant, **Massachusetts Hall** (1720), now houses both administrators and freshman dormitories. During the Revolution it served as barracks for Continental Army soldiers. Other colonial Harvard buildings include **Holden Chapel** (1744), **Harvard Hall** (1642, 1764) and **Hollis Hall** (1763).

Longfellow National Historic Site, 1759. (National Park Service)

Many college buildings were appropriated as housing by Continental Army soldiers during the Revolution, which displaced students. Therefore, Harvard College moved temporarily from Cambridge to Concord in October 1775. Harvard's move west was mostly due to the efforts of Ralph Waldo Emerson's grandfather, Concord minister William Emerson (both were Harvard graduates). After volunteering to serve as an army chaplain, William Emerson died of "camp fever" at Ruland, Vermont, in 1776, after accompanying colonial soldiers marching to reinforce Fort Ticonderoga on Lake Champlain. (Wheeler)

Longfellow National Historic Site (Vassall-Craigie-Longfellow House, 1759) is an imposing large yellow colonial mansion on "Tory Row" at 105 Brattle Street. It was originally the home of wealthy plantation owner John Vassall, Jr., whose loyalist sentiments prompted him to flee to England during the Revolution after the provisional government expropriated his house. George Washington used it as his headquarters in 1775–1776. Here he and Martha celebrated their seventeenth wedding anniversary in January 1776. Because former owner Andrew Craigie's insolvent widow was forced to take in boarders, in 1836, Henry Wadsworth Longfellow, a young Harvard professor, rented a room from widow Craigie. Longfellow later received the house as a wedding gift from the father of his bride, Fanny Appleton. The couple raised six children during their forty-five years as residents there. Longfellow's epic poems won him international fame. Longfellow House is operated by the National Park Service and is open to the public at regular hours and for special programs. Entry is free.

Other Brattle Street "Tory Row" houses include the **Henry Vassall House** (c. 1630s) at 94 Brattle Street and the **William Brattle House** (1727) at number 42. These houses are privately owned and not open to the public.

✷ Sources ✷

Batchelder, Samuel F. "The Washington Elm Tradition." *Cambridge Tribune,* 1925.

Bunting, Bainbridge, and Robert Nylander. *Old Cambridge.* Cambridge Historical Commission, 1998.

Cambridge Historical Commission. *A Brief History of Cambridge.* Cambridge Historical Commission, 1999.

Fleming, Thomas. *Liberty! The American Revolution.* New York: Viking, 1997.

Galvin, John R. *The Minutemen; The First Fight: Myths and Realities of the American Revolution.* Washington: Brassey's, 1967, 1989.

Harvard University. *A Self-Guided Walking Tour of the Harvard Yard.* Cambridge: Harvard University, 1998.

Ketchum, Richard M. *The World of George Washington.* New York: American Heritage, 1974.

Krim, Arthur J. *Northwest Cambridge.* Cambridge: Cambridge Historical Commission, 1977.

Longfellow National Historic Site, informational materials. Cambridge: 1999.

Okie, Susan, and Donna Yee (eds.). *Boston Bicentennial Guidebook.* Boston: Dutton, 1975.

Rees, James C. Opening of "George Washington: Portrait of a Patriot," sponsored by Mount Vernon Ladies' Association. Concord Museum, March 12, 1999.

Washington, George. *Maxims.* Virginia: reprinted by Mount Vernon Ladies' Association, 1989.

Wheeler, Ruth R. *Concord: Climate for Freedom.* Concord: Concord Antiquarian Society, 1967.

Arlington: The Battle Road's Most Savage Fighting

★ ★ ★ ★ ★ ★ ★ ★ ★ ★ ★ ★ ★ ★ ★ ★

On April 19, 1775, British soldiers were dispatched from Boston by governor and commanding general Thomas Gage. They marched, heading west toward Concord, to seize hidden colonial arms and supplies. Some four miles from Boston they reached a village called Menotomy. (Menotomy is a Native American word for "swift running waters." The town was once named West Cambridge and is now called Arlington.) As the soldiers marched through at about 3:00 A.M., all appeared quiet, although unusual stirrings were noted. Such would not be true later in the afternoon when the Redcoats returned.

Colonel Francis Smith's British column paused at Menotomy Center, near the Black Horse Tavern, which previously had hosted the illegal Provincial Committees of Safety and Supplies. A hungry British patrol had eaten there on the previous day. British major John Pitcairn was ordered to proceed with six companies to secure the bridges in Concord. These light infantry units later encountered and fired upon Captain John Parker's Lexington militia on the Lexington Common. By dawn, twenty-three of the fifty-three Menotomy Minute Men in Captain Benjamin Locke's company mustered and marched toward Lexington. Throughout the day, they would engage the king's soldiers at many points along what is now called the Battle Road.

By noon, following the deadly dawn skirmishes in Lexington and Concord, Colonel Smith's British forces began the long march back to Boston, harassed all along the way by provincials. As they were being battered at the "Bloody Angle" in Lincoln (at 1:30 P.M.), British brigadier general Hugh Lord Percy's relief brigade, previously summoned from Boston by a desperate Lieutenant Colonel Smith, was passing through a peaceful Menotomy. Somewhat behind the soldiers came two supply wagons, rushing to catch the column. They were ambushed by twelve Menotomy "old men" who had been left behind because they were considered unsuited for regular military duty. These men, led by a half-Indian named David Lamson, killed two British guards, wounded another, and captured the British supplies.

Fleeing British soldiers threw their muskets into Spy Pond, then surrendered to an old woman digging dandelions, Mother Ruth Bathericke. She presented her prisoners to a militia officer and informed the Redcoats, "If you ever live to get back, you tell King George that an old woman took six of his grenadiers prisoners." In England, newspapers asked, "If one old Yankee woman can take six grenadiers, how many soldiers will it require to conquer America?"

Colonel Smith's fleeing soldiers and the reinforcements from Boston under General Percy joined together in Lexington, creating a formidable force. They resumed their march together eastward toward Boston, entering Menotomy at about 4:30 P.M. near Foot of the Rocks (Arlington Heights). Colonial general William Heath and Dr. Joseph Warren had arrived on the field in an attempt to organize the provincials. Now the most savage, deadly, and intense combat of the day commenced, as some seventeen hundred Redcoats faced about two thousand rebels in thirty-five companies from Middlesex, Essex, and Norfolk counties in Massachusetts.

While the colonials fought independently and with minimal organization, the Regulars struggled to maintain discipline and order. Scared, tired, and angry, the British soldiers lost control, burning and looting houses they

Menotomy Minute Men and British Redcoats reenact the fierce fighting at the Jason Russell House in Arlington. (Menotomy Minute Men)

Headstone of Jason Russell, which also marks the resting place of eleven other Minute Men. (Arlington Historical Society)

believed had been used by colonials to fire upon them. Hannah Adams, baby in her arms and children under her bed, was assaulted at bayonet point but released. Her children managed to extinguish a fire set by the Redcoats. The Robbins and Cutler homes were vandalized and torched, and church silver was stolen.

Individual combat took place. Dr. Eliphalet Downer of Roxbury crossed bayonets with a Redcoat and killed him. Lieutenant Bowman of Menotomy caught a British straggler, clubbed him to the ground, and captured him. Samuel Whittemore, age 80, hid behind a wall with a musket, two pistols, and a sword. Upon being approached by British flankers, he killed two and wounded one before being knocked unconscious by a musket ball to his head. Battered, bayoneted, and left for dead by the soldiers, he was treated by Dr. Cotton Tufts, who believed the injured man could not survive. Whittemore, however, lived to the age of 98.

The most savage combat of the day took place at the farmhouse of Jason Russell. Age 58 and lame, Russell had refused to flee, noting that "an Englishman's house is his castle." When surprised by a British flanking party, a group of colonials sought refuge in Russell's house. Russell himself was too slow to escape and was shot twice then bayoneted eleven times by pursuing Redcoats. He died in his own doorway. Inside and about the building, thirteen provincials were killed, including seven from Danvers and four from Lynn. Two Regulars were killed. Eight colonials saved themselves by hiding in the cellar, which the Redcoats dared not enter. Mrs. Russell, upon returning home, noted bodies piled about the floor and blood ankle deep.

At Cooper's Tavern, the owner Benjamin Cooper and his wife fled to the cellar as the British soldiers approached. However, two unarmed noncombatants, believing themselves safe from harm, continued drinking their ale. Jason Winship and Jabez Wyman were bayoneted to death, their heads mauled, their skulls broken, and their brains scattered about the floor and walls.

Just after 6:00 P.M., as the sun set in the west, the British column passed quietly out of war-torn, smoldering Menotomy into Cambridge. During the one and a half hours that they had traveled along the almost two miles of the

Menotomy road, unimaginable horrors had occurred, accounting for almost half of the day's casualties on both sides. Twenty-eight colonists of the total of forty-nine killed that day along the Battle Road were slain in Menotomy. Ten more were wounded, out of the total of forty-one wounded.

Forty Redcoats were killed, out of the total of seventy-three deaths along the Battle Road, and about eighty were wounded out of the 174 total British soldiers wounded on that day.

The twelve colonials killed at Jason Russell's house were buried in a mass grave behind the First Parish Church. British lieutenant Edward Gould, wounded in Concord, was captured in Menotomy. Lieutenant Edward Hall, also wounded in Concord, was again hit and died in the village. He was treated by Mrs. Butterfield, who was called a Tory for her actions, but later defended her act of humanity. Lieutenant Joseph Knight died of wounds received in town. One British soldier noted, "We were most annoyed at a village called Anatomy [sic] . . . houses were all full of men."

Menotomy bled and burned in the fury of battle on April 19, 1775, and its citizens spilled their blood to defend ideals and help begin a revolution. Then the events of that day in their town quietly disappeared into history, overshadowed by the more famous combat that day at Concord and Lexington. In an odd but hopeful twist of fate, the granddaughter of the slain Jason Russell was born in Menotomy Village on that very same fateful day, and on the next sabbath, the infant son of Jason Winship was baptized. After all the carnage of April 19, a new generation was being born to ensure Menotomy's future.

Jason Russell House, 1740. (Author)

The **Jason Russell House** (1740) and **Smith History Museum** at 7 Jason Street near Massachusetts Avenue and Route 60, is operated by the Arlington Historical Society and open to the public at specified times. It occupies the site of fierce hand-to-hand combat during the British retreat to Boston. Now it houses eighteenth-century furniture and artifacts as well as changing exhibits about the Revolutionary War.

First Parish Church and Burial Ground at 638 Massachusetts Avenue near Route 60 are open to the public.

Spy Pond, where the fleeing British troops tossed their muskets, provided cut ice later in the 1830s, which was shipped to help to cool tropical countries as distant as India. It can be viewed from Route 2 driving west or from Route 60 driving north.

Foot of the Rocks, at the corner of Lowell and Massachusetts Avenues in Arlington Heights, is marked by boulders with plaques, commemorating the spot where the deadliest combat occurred on April 19, 1775, between retreating British troops and colonial soldiers from over thirty neighboring towns.

Captain Benjamin Locke's house at 21 Appleton Street in Arlington Heights and the Whittemore House at 54 Massachusetts Avenue in East Arlington previously housed the families of participants in the Menotomy skirmish. The houses are now privately owned and not open to the public.

The **Minute Man Bike Trail**, originally an abandoned rail line, starts in East Arlington and runs 11.2 miles through Lexington to Bedford. It is popular with cyclists and strollers in the summer and with cross-country skiers when snow falls.

The Menotomy Minute Men were reorganized in 1971 to perpetuate the memory and achievements of the original company through living history reenactments, educational programs, and promotion of civic events. The company consists of musketeers, a fife and drum corps, and the Menotomy Boys and Girls groups. Membership is open to interested individuals and families.

—D. Michael Ryan

✹ Sources ✹

First National Bank of Boston. *The Lexington-Concord Battle Road.* 1975.
French, Allen. *The Day of Concord and Lexington.* 1925.
Smith, Samuel. *West Cambridge 1775.* 1974.

Lincoln: The Battle Road Runs Through It

★ ★ ★ ★ ★ ★ ★ ★ ★ ★ ★ ★ ★ ★ ★ ★ ★ ★

The town of Lincoln, lying between Lexington and Concord, contains a long segment of the original Battle Road—the road along which the British passed on their retreat to Boston. The National Park Service has restored this section of the Battle Road to its appearance in 1775 (as much as modern conditions permit).

In the 1770s, Lincoln was a farming community of only 750 residents; most were Patriots, but a few were Tories. As political tensions with the British government grew, the voters of Lincoln agreed in January 1775 to raise a company of Minute Men at the urging of the Massachusetts Provincial Congress. Yet in true Yankee fashion, the town did not vote to pay for them until three months later, on March 20:

"Voted as followes that the Sum of fifty-two Pounds four Shillings be and is hereby granted to provide for those persons who have inlisted as minute men each one a bayonet belt Catrige Box Steal ramer gun stock and knap sack; they to attend military Exercise four hours in a day twice in a week . . . the officers to keep an exact account of their attendance." (MacLean)

Under colonial laws dating to the seventeenth century, all males between the ages of sixteen and forty-five were required to be members of the militia, and Lincoln had a regular militia company. The wisdom of preparing a portion of the militia to march "at a moment's notice," as well as the name "Minute Men," were also old ideas, and Lincoln's elder veterans from the French and Indian War (1754–1760) knew what was required. The town raised a company of sixty-two Minute Men, the majority of them young and sturdy farmers' sons, unmarried and living with their parents. They elected William Smith as their captain. He was only twenty-nine years old, and he had no battlefield experience. His first lieutenant, Samuel Farrar, Jr., was a more mature thirty-nine, but Farrar had no battle experience either. (Many of Lincoln's older community leaders had already accepted higher positions in the Massachusetts militia.) Smith was one of the largest property holders in

Nineteenth-century photo of the Battle Road in Lincoln. (Concord Free Public Library)

town, and he was the brother-in-law of John Adams, the patriot leader and future president.

In Lincoln, the events of April 19, 1775, began with Paul Revere's capture and an uncommon act of bravery by Mary Flint Hartwell, wife of a sergeant of the Lincoln Minute Men. When Revere and his companions, William Dawes and Dr. Samuel Prescott, were intercepted in Lincoln by a British patrol at about one o'clock in the morning while attempting to carry the alarm to Concord, Prescott escaped by galloping his horse through a neighboring swamp. When he returned to the road farther on and awakened the Hartwell family, Samuel Hartwell made ready to join his Minute Man unit while Mary walked into the night—and toward the British patrol—to carry the alarm to their neighbor, Captain William Smith. Then Smith rode to the town center, rang the meetinghouse bell, and ordered the Lincoln Minute Men to head for Concord. Soon Minute Men and militia members converged on Lincoln's country roads and marched in defense of American liberty. In 1850, Amos Baker, a private in Lincoln's militia and the last surviving participant in the battle at the North Bridge, would recall the scene: "When I went to Concord in the morning, I joined the Lincoln company at the brook, by Flint's pond.

. . . I loaded my gun there with two balls, ounce balls, and powder accordingly." The Lincoln Minute Men and militia were the first units from neighboring towns to reach Concord that April morning.

An incident at the North Bridge involving a Lincoln militiaman calls to mind how divided communities were over the dispute with Great Britain. James Nichols was a recent immigrant from England and a farmer in Lincoln, well liked as "a good droll fellow and a fine singer." But as he watched the Redcoats assembled at the bridge, he suddenly said to the men standing near him, "If any of you will hold my gun, I will go down and talk with them." He walked down the hill to the British soldiers and spoke with them briefly. Then he returned to his militia company, retrieved his musket, and announced that he was going home. (Fischer, 209) How well James Nichols fared afterward in the small town of Lincoln we can only guess. Months later, however, his neighbors accepted him back into the Lincoln militia, which was then helping lay siege to the British in Boston. But not long afterward, Nichols deserted to the British side and was not heard from again.

✯ REVOLUTIONARY WAR SITES TO VISIT TODAY IN LINCOLN ✯

A stone monument and plaque at the **Paul Revere Capture Site** (1775) mark the approximate place where this historic event occurred. All that survives of the **Samuel and Mary Flint Hartwell House**, which was almost destroyed by a fire in later years, is the cellar and an elaborate chimney studded with fireplaces, but those remnants provide a view of the sturdy skeleton of a typical New England colonial house. Nearby, the **William Smith House** (1693) and the **Hartwell Tavern** (1733), which was run by Samuel's father, have been restored by the Minute Man National Historical Park and are open to visitors and staffed by historical interpreters.

The segment of the **Battle Road** (now Route 2A) that runs through Lincoln is only two and a half miles long. Yet so intense was the fighting along this stretch that the retreating British soldiers nearly exhausted their ammunition and their discipline there. The skirmishes at Lexington Green (at 5:00 A.M.) and Concord's North Bridge (at about 9:30 A.M.) had resulted in deaths and great anger on both sides, but they had not yet provoked a sustained battle. All that would change in Lincoln.

In early afternoon, just to the west of town at **Meriam's Corner** in Concord, the militias gathering from towns near and far now outnumbered the Redcoats, and they began to form in battle lines. As the British column marched past on its return eastward to Boston, a sharp exchange of musket fire occurred, and several British soldiers fell, dead and wounded. The Redcoats tried to move more briskly as they crossed into Lincoln, but again and again the colonists formed deadly ambushes in the woods and behind the piled

Colonial reenactors at Hartwell Tavern, bvilt in 1733. (Author)

stone walls that lined the road—at Brook's Hill, at the curves in the road now called **Bloody Angle**, and around the barn and buildings of Samuel and Mary Hartwell's farm. The colonial troops aimed especially at the British officers, creating great disorder among the troops. And further to the east, at the Lexington boundary, militiamen from Lincoln joined with Captain John Parker's men of Lexington in yet another ambush, this one in revenge for the killings on Lexington Common that morning. As it left Lincoln, the British column was disintegrating into a running mob, pursued now by several thousand colonials.

Ten British soldiers were killed along the road in Lincoln, eight of them within yards of the Hartwell home. The morning after the battle, as Mary Hartwell later recounted,

> The men hitched the oxen to the cart . . . and gathered up the dead. As they returned with the team and the dead soldiers, my thoughts went out for the wives, parents, and children across the Atlantic, who would never again see their loved ones; and I left the house, and taking my little children by the hand, I followed the rude hearse to the grave hastily made in the burial ground. I remember how cruel it seemed to put them into one large trench without any coffins. There was one in a brilliant uniform, whom I supposed to have been an officer. (MacLean)

In 1884, the citizens of Lincoln placed a **memorial stone** over the British gravesite in the old town cemetery on Lexington Road in Lincoln. Each April, to the sound of muffled drums, fifes, and bagpipe, the modern Lincoln Minutemen assemble with Redcoat units to commemorate the sacrifices of these soldiers and of the Lincoln Revolutionary War heroes (including Mary Hartwell) who are buried nearby. Visitors to the old town cemetery will find these graves marked by small flags.

The **original Lincoln town center**, at the intersection of Trapelo and Bedford roads, retains much of the charm of a New England farm community, with houses and buildings dating to the eighteenth and early nineteenth centuries, clustered around a white church built in the traditional New England style. All that remains of the original meetinghouse where Captain Smith rang the alarm is an old graveyard, where the stones bear the names of many of Lincoln's Revolutionary War soldiers. Standing amidst these graves and gazing northward in the direction of the Battle Road, past the houses and barns and open fields, a visitor with a lively imagination might still hear the fife and drum and the crackle of musket fire—and the birth of American independence.

On April 19, 2000, the people of Lincoln placed two stone markers to memorialize locations where the Minute Men and militia mustered in 1775. One is on the common at town center and the other at Dakin's Field (intersection of Sandy Pond and Baker Bridge Road). Each stone is inscribed with the site's role on April 19, 1775.

—Donald L. Hafner

✯ SOURCES ✯

Brooks, Paul. *The View from Lincoln Hill.* Boston: Houghton Mifflin, 1976.

Fischer, David Hackett. *Paul Revere's Ride.* New York: Oxford, 1994.

Hersey, Frank W. *Heroes of the Battle Road.* Boston: Perry Walton, 1930.

MacLean, John C. *A Rich Harvest: The History, Buildings, and People of Lincoln, Massachusetts.* Lincoln Historical Society, 1987.

Bedford's Contributions
to the Cause

★ ★ ★ ★ ★ ★ ★ ★ ★ ★ ★ ★ ★ ★ ★ ★ ★

G et up, Nat Page! The Regulars are out!" The knocking on his door was persistent. Nathaniel Page, a young Bedford Minute Man, was roused out of bed abruptly before dawn on April 19, 1775. The alarm message had been sent by Captain John Parker in Lexington and carried by Nathan Monroe and Benjamin Tidd on their fleet horses. They galloped to Bedford, where they stopped at Page's house first. Page headed for the Fitch Tavern, less than a half mile away. (Brown, Fischer)

At the time Bedford was a small farming village of 482 people, northwest of Boston. The Bedford Minute Men gathered first at Fitch Tavern in Bedford's center for a hurried breakfast of cold cornmeal mush. Their leader, Captain Jonathan Wilson, was reported to have said, "It's a cold breakfast, boys, but we'll give the British a hot dinner. We'll have every dog of them before night!" The men mustered under a spreading oak at the junction of Concord, Lexington, and North roads, near today's Wilson Park.

One half mile down the Concord Road, the fifty-man Bedford militia company, commanded by John Moore, had already departed and was headed for Concord's Wright Tavern six miles away. Many men in the militia were veterans who had fought with the British army in the French and Indian War, which ended in 1763. Some in town doubted the veterans' loyalty to the rebel cause in the event of an actual armed conflict, since they were on King George's payroll. But they were to prove their total support for the patriots' cause later that day.

Bedford's fifty militiamen were soon to joined by twenty-seven Bedford Minute Men in Concord. Together, Bedford's seventy-seven farmer-soldiers formed about a fifth of the total colonial force, the largest contingent of any town that gathered on Punkatasset Hill overlooking the North Bridge at dawn, awaiting the arrival of the British troops. The Bedford men followed the men of Acton and Concord down the hill at about 9:30 A.M. to clash with the British at the North Bridge.

Bedford's contribution to the pursuit of the British army along the Battle Road from Concord to Boston is described as follows by Abram Brown: "Bedford men were in pursuit of the retreating enemy. They left the Great Fields at Meriams Corner, and engaged in the attack, then hastened in the pursuit, and were in the thickest of the fight near Brook's Tavern [in Lincoln], where Captain Wilson was killed and Job Lane wounded." Job Lane of the militia, whose house can be visited today, was crippled by the musket ball that hit his hip.

Maxwell Thompson, a drover who was related to Captain Wilson by marriage, wrote later that he had joined the Concord Fight in April and did not return to his home in Bedford until after the Battle of Bunker Hill in June. Apparently, many other Bedford citizen-soldiers did the same, joining the newly assembled Continential Army that would surround the British in the siege of Boston.

In 1964, a company of Bedford Minutemen was reestablished by the Bedford board of selectmen to keep alive the spirit of 1775. The company adopted a uniform similar to those worn by officers in Washington's Continental Army. They march at events to commemorate Bedford's rich Revolutionary heritage. (Farrington)

★ THE BEDFORD FLAG ★

Perhaps no other historical artifact relating the Revolutionary War in the Boston area is more a soure of local pride—and of controversy—than the Bedford Flag. Oral tradition has it that when the alarm went out on the night of April 18, 1775, young Nathaniel Page, a Bedford Minute Man, took a flag from its honored position in the Page home and carried it the following morning into the skirmish at Old North Bridge. Oral tradition within the Page family (especially the claims of Nathaniel's grandson Cyrus) and the work of Bedford historians seem to substantiate this belief. (Hitchcock, McDonald, MacLaughlan, Filios) To this day, on April 19 each year, the lead man in Concord's parade is a Bedford Minute Man in full dress uniform, bearing this very Bedford Flag.

Skeptics, such as historian D. Michael Ryan, point out that no contemporary accounts report the flag's being carried at the Concord Fight. They conclude that the Bedford Flag never was at the April 19, 1775, battle.

Historical and scientific evidence has been mustered on each side of the argument. Here is what we *do* know about the banner known today as the Bedford Flag.

Analysis of the flag's fabric and paint has led experts to conclude that it is pure silk damask dating from the early eighteenth century. The red design shows a mailed (armored) arm emerging from a cloud and grasping a sword.

The Bedford Flag, displayed by Jan van Steenwijk, Barbara Hitchcock, and a member of the Bedford Minutemen. (Author)

The Latin inscription reads, *Vince Aut Morire* (Conquer or Die).

This flag was kept in the Page family for many years after the Revolution and presented to the town in 1875. It was flown in Concord on April 19, 1875, during the centennial celebration of the Concord Fight. Its last appearance in Concord was a dramatic one. On April 19, 1925, World War I doughboy veterans from Bedford displayed the venerated flag from an open car driven through the streets of Concord. Copies of the Bedford Flag may be seen at several Boston area sites, including Minute Man National Historical Park and the Ancient and Honorable Artillery Armory Museum in Faneuil Hall. The recently rehabilitated Page family flag is on display at the Bedford Public Library.

✯ REVOLUTIONARY WAR SITES TO VISIT TODAY IN BEDFORD ✯

Job Lane House (c. 1713) at 295 North Road is one of Bedford's earliest homes. Built in the saltbox style to house Lane's eleven children, it was enlarged by succeeding generations in different period styles, including Georgian and Federal. The home stayed in the Lane family for over 130 years. Since 1973, it has been owned by the town of Bedford. In a creative approach to the challenge of affordably preserving a historic building, many Bedford organizations have each adopted a room, which they help to restore and maintain. These groups include the Bedford Minutemen, the Historical Society, the Garden Club, the Rotary, the Boy Scouts, and the Girl Scouts. Friends of the Job Lane House conduct guided tours from May to October on alternate Sunday afternoons.

Fitch Tavern (c. 1731) on Great Road near Town Hall is where the Bedford Minute Men rallied at dawn on April 19, 1775, before marching to the battle at Concord's North Bridge. The building is privately owned and not open to the public.

—John E. Filios and Joseph L. Andrews, Jr.

☆ Sources ☆

Brown, Abram E. *History of Bedford.* Boston: 1891.

————. *Beneath Old Rooftrees.* Boston: 1896.

Brown, L. K., *Wilderness Town.* Bedford: 1968.

Farrington, Williston. *The Flag of the Minutemen.* Bedford: Bedford Minuteman Company, 1996.

Filios, John. "The Bedford Flag." Unpublished essay, 2001.

Fischer, David H. *Paul Revere's Ride.* New York: Oxford, 1994.

Hitchcock, Barbara. *The Bedford Flag: A National Treasure.* Bedford: Friends of the Bedford Flag, 1998.

MacLaughlan, James E., and Reader, David B. "The Bedford Flag, The First Flag of the United States." Bedford: 1975.

McDonald, Sharon. "The Bedford Flag" (brochure). Bedford Free Public Library, 1995.

Ryan, D. Michael. Personal communication with the authors.

Wharton, Virginia. *The Bedford Sampler: Centennial Edition.* Bedford: 1974.

Acton: "I Haven't a Man Who is Afraid to Go!"

★ ★ ★ ★ ★ ★ ★ ★ ★ ★ ★ ★ ★ ★ ★ ★

On the morning of April 19, 1775, believing that British troops were setting fire to the town of Concord, colonial officers ordered their militia and Minute Men to advance across the North Bridge toward the waiting muskets of the British. Colonel James Barrett instructed Major John Buttrick to find a company to take the lead in this dangerous endeavor. He asked a Concord captain, who declined. Buttrick then asked Acton's Captain Isaac Davis, who was heard to reply, "I haven't a man who is afraid to go!" The brave actions of Captain Davis and his men at this crucial juncture in American history led subsequent generations of Acton residents to characterize the events of the day as "the Battle of Lexington, fought in Concord, by men of Acton."

Acton's defiance of the British Crown had slowly gathered momentum in the preceding years. In 1772 Acton men replied to Boston's Committee of Correspondence, noting alarming violations of the colonists' royal charter of rights and privileges. They petitioned for the removal of British governor Thomas Hutchinson, who personified their grievances. In 1773, after the Boston Tea Party protest, Acton and other Massachusetts towns passed resolutions condemning the actions of the Crown.

On October 3, 1774, a special Acton town meeting chose delegates for the First Provincial Congress. This congress was held in defiance of Parliament, which had passed the retaliatory Coercive (of "Intolerable") Acts. By sending delegates to the Provincial Congress, Acton defied the royal governor in Boston who was charged with enforcing the restrictions. These new measures banned town meetings, which colonists felt were among their most treasured rights as Englishmen, rights guaranteed by royal charter. Thus October 3, 1774, was a crucial turning point—the day Acton cast its lot with other patriots against Parliament and the royal governor in Boston. Crown Resistance Day, celebrated in Acton for many years on October 3, is now honored by the Acton Minute Men on the last weekend in September.

"Minutemen Leaving the Home of Captain Isaac Davis, April 19, 1775, in Acton" by Acton artist Arthur Fuller Davis, 1894. (Acton Historical Society)

In 1775 Acton was a farming village of approximately 750 people with two companies of militia and volunteers who formed one company of Minute Men.In theory the militia companies, under the command of Colonel Francis Faulkner and Captain Joseph Robbins, were under orders from the Crown (because Faulkner's and Robbins's commissions came from the royal governor). In practice, as the years passed, this ceased to be reality.

In November 1774, a company of Minute Men was organized in Acton through volunteer enlistment. Isaac Davis, a gunsmith by trade, was elected captain. Davis's Minute Man company was particularly noted for its zeal. It met twice weekly for drill, to the accompaniment of fifes and drums.

On the fateful morning of April 19, 1775, Concord's Dr. Samuel Prescott escaped after being captured by British soldiers in Lincoln on the road from Lexington. Galloping furiously, he spread the alarm to Concord at about 2:00 A.M., and then to Acton and Stow at about 2:00 or 3:00 A.M. Prescott's first stop in Acton was the home of Captain Joseph Robbins. He did not dismount but pounded against the clapboards and shouted, "Captain Robbins, Captain Robbins! The Regulars are coming!" He then raced on to alert Colonel Francis Faulkner in South Acton, and thence to neighboring Stow.

Captain Robbins rushed from the house with his musket and fired three shots as rapidly as he could reload. This was the signal for each Acton Minute Man and militiaman to report to the home of his captain, armed and prepared to march to Concord. The alarm was picked up, and the sound of three musket shots could soon be heard repeated across the countryside. John Robbins, the captain's thirteen-year-old son, mounted the family mare and rode off, carrying the news to Captain Davis and to Captain Simon Hunt, who led the Faulkner company.

Thirty-seven Acton Minute Men arrived at Captain Davis's house before dawn on April 19, 1775, each outfitted with musket and bayonet, powder horn, bullet pouch, and a ration of bread and cheese. The march to Concord began to the familiar tune of "The White Cockade," or so the story is told.

The British expedition of about seven hundred Redcoats, marching from Boston and Lexington, had already reached Concord. A British raiding force was ordered to cross the Concord River at the North Bridge and to proceed to Barrett's farm to seize weapons and burn supplies that, according to information from spies, were hidden in Colonel Barrett's barn. While the colonials watched from their vantage point on Punkatasset Hill, seven companies of British Regulars reached the North Bridge. Four of these companies crossed the bridge and proceeded to Barrett's farm two miles distant, while the other three companies remained to guard the bridge.

The last time all local Minute Man companies had mustered was in March on Concord's common. As Captain Davis and his men reached Barrett's Mill Road in Concord on the fateful day, they were told that Colonel James Barrett, in general command of the militia at Concord, had ordered his men to Punkatasset Hill above the west side of the Concord River, overlooking the North Bridge. Marching to that location, Acton Minute Men found the colonial force formed in a field at Buttrick's farm. As on muster days, the companies took up their positions, militia on the left, Minute Man companies on the right (the place of honor), facing the North Bridge.

Soon after the arrival of Acton's Minute Men, the colonial officers called the first council of war in what was to become the American Revolution. Colonel Barrett was in command. Rumors and reports of shooting in Lexington earlier that morning were spreading, but the stories were confused and unverified. As the officers conferred, the assembled colonial militiamen saw smoke rising below, over the town of Concord. Thinking the British were setting fire to their homes, the colonial officers decided to cross the North Bridge to save the town.

Colonel Barrett ordered Major John Buttrick to have his soldiers march down the hill and toward the bridge and into the town, but not to fire unless fired upon. It was then that Captain Davis agreed to have his men take the lead. (In later years a soldier who was at the scene claimed that the Acton men were placed in the front ranks because they were the only company equipped with bayonets. He claimed the Acton men were also the best trained and followed the most dynamic leader.) Davis's company marched toward the bridge, followed by two Minute Man companies from Concord, the Bedford and Lincoln Minute Man companies, and then the Hunt and Robbins companies from Acton along with other militia companies.

Dedication of the Isaac Davis Monument in Acton center, October 29, 1851. (Acton Historical Society)

As the colonists approached, the British Redcoats posted on the west side of the Concord River retreated east over the North Bridge. A few Regulars began to take up the planks from the bridge, which were not nailed down. Major Buttrick shouted at them to stop. The British fell back with their comrades to the east bank of the river to form a line for firing their muskets. When the column of patriots was near the bridge, the Redcoats fired a few random warning shots followed by a volley. One ball creased the forehead of Luther Blanchard, the Acton fifer, slightly wounding him and a Concord militiaman in the ranks behind. Major Buttrick then gave the order to the colonists to return fire: "Fire, fellow soldiers; for God's sake, fire!"

The Acton men led the citizen-soldiers in the front ranks and thus were the only colonials in a position to fire. As they lifted their muskets, the British fired a volley and Acton's Isaac Davis was killed instantly. Abner Hosmer, also of Acton, was mortally wounded with a bullet through his head. Thus the Acton men, who had volunteered to lead the colonists in what was later dubbed "the first forcible resistance to British aggression," also gained the distinction of becoming the only patriots killed at the skirmish at North Bridge, later known as the Concord Fight.

The volley returned by the Minute Men killed one Redcoat, fatally wounded two others, and wounded several more, including four British officers. While British retreated to the town center, the colonists became somewhat disorganized. About two hundred gathered on Ripley Hill to watch the British, but most of the others returned across the bridge. The bodies of Davis and Hosmer were carried up the hill to Major Buttrick's home and then returned to Acton later that day.

Isaac Davis's widow, Hannah, who was left with four children, the youngest about fifteeen months of age, described that fateful day in a deposition sixty years later:

> The alarm was given early in the morning, and my husband lost no time in making ready to go to Concord.
>
> My husband said but little that morning. He seemed serious and thoughtful; but never seemed to hesitate as to the course of his duty. As he led the company from the house, he turned himself round and seemed to have something to communicate. He said only, "Take good care of the children," and was soon out of sight.
>
> In the afternoon he was brought home a corpse. He was placed in my bedroom till the funeral. His countenance was pleasant and seemed little altered.
>
> The bodies of Abner Hosmer, one of the company, and of James Hayward, one of the militia company, who was killed in Lexington [later that afternoon] were brought by their friends to the house, where the funeral of the three was attended together. (Deposition of the widow of Captain Davis before Justice of the Peace Francis Tuttle, August 14, 1835)

As the war progressed, more Acton men enlisted. Twenty-three were at Bunker Hill on June 17, 1775. Josiah Hayward was sent to represent the town in the Provincial Congress, which began to prepare for a long campaign. By December, quotas of military supplies were assigned to various towns. Acton was required to supply a ton of hay, ten blankets, and thirteen more men.

In the spring of 1776 the idea of independence from England spread through the colonies. The redress of grievances and a guarantee of civil rights were no longer enough. Acton voters went on record in their town meeting of June 14, 1776, as believing that "the present age will be Defiant in their duty to God, their posterity, and themselves if they Do not Establish an American Republic."

☆ REVOLUTIONARY ERA SITES TO VISIT TODAY IN ACTON ☆

The **Hosmer House** (1760), 300 Main Street, is a restored saltbox farmhouse. It was built for Jonathan Hosmer, a bricklayer, and his bride, Submit Hunt. Hosmer's younger brother Abner was killed at the North Bridge fight in 1775. The farmhouse was enlarged for the Hosmers' son Simon and his wife, Sarah, in 1797. Owned and operated by the Acton Historical Society, it is open to the public for teas and tours on a limited basis.

The **Jenks Library**, also at 300 Main Street behind the Hosmer House, contains the Acton Historical Society's archives, including papers, maps, and pictures. It is open to the public on Monday and Wednesday mornings, or by appointment.

The **Faulkner Homestead** (1707) at 5 High Street is the oldest house still standing in Acton. It was the house of Colonel Francis Faulkner, who commanded one of Acton's three military companies. In the front yard of the house, Acton's provincial militia mustered and then marched off to the Concord Fight on April 19, 1775. It was the homestead for six generations of the Faulkner family over the course of 202 years (1728–1940). Today it is owned by the Iron Work Farm of Acton, a historic preservation organization, and is open the fourth Sunday of the month or by appointment.

The **Isaac Davis Monument** (1851), on Main Street in Acton Center on the green opposite Town Hall, is a tall stone obelisk. At its base are buried the three Acton men killed on April 19, 1775, Captain Isaac Davis and Abner Hosmer (both slain at Concord's North Bridge) and James Hayward (later killed in Lexington). Their bodies were moved here from burying grounds elsewhere in Acton at an elaborate dedication ceremony in 1851.

Acton residents continue to honor their rich heritage. The Acton Minutemen of today march in commemoration of Captain Isaac Davis and his company of thirty-eight men. The group was reactivated as the Acton Militia in 1963 and takes part in many town and area celebrations.

Each year on April 19 the Acton Minutemen again march along the original trail from the Davis homestead to the Concord bridge, a distance of about eight miles. In recent years they have been followed by thousands of participants, including American servicemen, area students, and Boy Scouts and Girl Scouts. Upon completing their trek on the **Isaac Davis Trail**, each marcher is awarded a scroll and a map of the historic route, commemorating the event. The Acton Minutemen then participate, along with uniformed Minute Men and militia units from many Massachusetts towns, in marching through the streets of Concord to the North Bridge in Concord's annual Patriots' Day Parade.

✯ SOURCES ✯

Conant, Elizabeth S., and David W. Stonecliffe (eds.). *A Brief History of Acton.* Acton: Acton Historical Society, 1974.

Hamlin, the Reverend Cyrus. *My Grandfather Colonel Francis Faulkner and My Uncle Francis Faulkner, Jr. in the Battle of Lexington.* Acton: 1887. (Reprinted in 1983.)

Fischer, David H. *Paul Revere's Ride.* New York: Oxford, 1994.

Sudbury's
April Morning

★ ★ ★ ★ ★ ★ ★ ★ ★ ★ ★ ★ ★ ★ ★ ★

Sudbury, a quiet farming community west of Boston, was incorporated as a town in 1639. It was named after the town of Sudbury in Suffolk, England. After events such as the terrible massacre in Boston during the cold winter night of March 5, 1770, and the British raid on the powderhouse in Somerville in September 1774, Sudbury citizens felt they needed to be ready to act in their own defense. They felt tensions building up between the colonists and the British crown. Accordingly, in November 1774, the citizens of Sudbury voted to recommend that the militia companies elect officers and hold them in readiness to protect the town and country against any aggression from British Regulars. Those companies and officers were:

- North Militia Company, West Side, Captain Aaron Haynes (60 men)
- East Militia Company, East Side, Captain Joseph Smith (75 men)
- South Militia Company, both sides, Captain Moses Stone (92 men)
- Troop of Horse, both sides, Captain Isaac Loker (21 men)
- Minute Company, West Side, Captain John Nixon (58 men)
- Minute Company, East Side, Captain Nathaniel Cudworth (40 men)
- Alarm Company, Captain Jabez Puffer (the men and boys who were too old or young to serve in the other companies)

All companies were under the command of Lieutenant Colonel Ezekiel How. By March 1775, most men were equipped with usable firelocks, flints, bayonets, one pound of powder, cartridge boxes, and about two pounds of lead—enough to make about thirty or so musket balls. Those not as well equipped carried pitchforks, hatchets, and even clubs. The colonists knew how to use their flintlocks as well as any Redcoat. During the cold winter months they drilled with mittens on, in barns. As a confrontation with the king's troops seemed to grow more inevitable, they drilled weekly and honed their shooting skills. They were ready.

Then it happened! During the early morning of April 19, 1775, between three o'clock and four o'clock in the morning, Abel Prescott, Jr., an alarm rider sent from Concord by his brother, Samuel Prescott, awoke Thomas Plympton, who lived in Sudbury Center. Plympton was a member of the Committee of Correspondence and the Provincial Congress. Plympton awoke the church sexton around 4:30 A.M. He instructed him to ring the alarm bell and discharge his musket. Another messenger woke Captain Nixon's household shouting, "Up, up! The Redcoats are up as far as Concord!"

By sunrise, Sudbury Center was a frenzy of activity. Alarm riders dashed off to warn other towns. Drummers beat out assembly as men fell into ranks. Wives and mothers helped husbands and sons with last-minute preparations. Dogs barked as horses stomped and snorted. Young men wondered what the day would bring. Others, veterans of the French and Indian War, knew full well that some of their neighbors might die shortly. Soon they were off. . . . Lieutenant Colonel How and Captains Nixon and Haynes led the north militia and Minute Men companies toward Concord to the sound of fifes and drums, which lifted spirits in the warm April morning. The east side Sudbury companies, in similar fashion, headed toward Concord by way of Lincoln.

As the companies led by Nixon and Haynes were within a half mile of the Concord South Bridge, they were intercepted by Stephen Barrett. Barrett was the son of Colonel James Barrett, commander of the Concord militia companies. Stephen Barrett said that companies of Redcoats were already holding the South Bridge. The Minute Men and militia companies were ordered to detour around the South Bridge and head toward Concord's North Bridge. As Lieutenant Colonel How spoke with his captains about the situation, eighty-year-old Deacon Josiah Haynes grew restless and said to Captain Nixon, "If you don't go and drive them British from the bridge, I shall call you a coward."

Trying to quell Haynes's impatience, Nixon replied, "I should rather be called a coward by you than called to account by my superiors for disobedience of orders." Cooler heads prevailed, and the companies detoured around South Bridge, avoiding an immediate conflict.

While on the way to the North Bridge, How's column approached the farmhouse of Colonel James Barrett. The Sudbury men spied four companies of British soldiers at Barrett's house. Those soldiers under the command of Captain Parsons had been ordered to search Barrett's home for hidden military stores. Finding some wooden gun carriages, the Redcoats dragged them to the front yard and set them ablaze. Upon seeing the blaze from a distance, Lieutenant Colonel How roared, "If any blood has been shed, not one of the rascals shall escape!"

Wanting a closer look, How removed his sword and ventured up to Barrett's house as if he was just passing by. Stopped by the British soldiers, he was asked where he was going. "Down along on some business and should not

The Wayside Inn in Sudbury, circa 1716. (Wayside Inn)

like to be detained," How stated matter-of-factly. The British soldiers, not suspecting him of any wrongdoing, let him pass. Seeing that no harm had come to the Barrett family, How proceeded along his way.

Seeing this, the Sudbury companies detoured around the Redcoats and met up with How. Smoke was seen rising from the direction of Concord Center, and minutes later shots were heard from the direction of the North Bridge. Still two miles from the bridge, How ordered his column to make haste toward the sound of the firing. British Captain Parsons ordered his troops to the town center.

As Captain Parsons approached the North Bridge, he passed a large group of colonials heading in the opposite direction. Upon reaching the bridge, where the smell of gunpowder still hung in the air, he observed that there had been a skirmish. He grasped the seriousness of the moment. Parsons thought the colonials might attack his rear. His men hastily headed for Concord Center. There was no colonial attack on Parsons's force.

By this time, Colonel How and his column had met up with the returning colonial troops on the muster ground above the North Bridge. The commanders assessed the situation, realizing the gravity of their action. There was no turning back!

After a rest of about two hours in Concord Center, the British column started their fateful march back to Boston. About half past twelve in the afternoon, at Meriam's Corner, as the British Regulars crossed a small bridge, shots supposedly were fired by a few Minute Men at the rear of the British column. The British guard turned and fired. In response to this volley, provincial muskets started sniping at the British column from all sides. Soldiers from East Sudbury, commanded by Captain Joseph Smith and situated on the south side of Meriam's Corner, joined in the firing. Two British soldiers were killed and several officers wounded, including Ensign Jeremy Lester.

About a mile and a half from Meriam's Corner, the British passed Brooks Tavern. British officer Lieutenant Sutherland stated, "Here I saw upon a height upon my right hand a vast number of armed men drawn out in Battalia order [battle line], I dare say near 1,000 who on our coming nearer dispersed into the woods." Nearly five hundred provincials from Framingham and the Sudbury company of Captain Nathaniel Cudworth engaged the British at Hardy's (Brooks) Hill. When the British charged up the hill toward the men hidden in the woods, deadly provincial musketry drove them back. Sudbury Minute Men and militiamen fought on both sides of the road at Hardy's Hill. One young man recalled, "I was running across a lot where there was a bend in [the] road in order to get a fair shot, at the enemy, in company with a Scotsman who was in Braddock's defeat 19 year before, after we had discharged our guns I observed the Scot who appeared very composed I wished I felt as calm as he appeared to be." The old Scot, named John Weighton, replied to the young lad, "It's a Tread to be Larnt." Weighton had already survived seven battles.

As the sun set on April 19, 1775, people reflected, buried their dead, and bandaged their wounded. Sudbury had lost two men. Feisty eighty-year-old Deacon Josiah Haynes, who dared call his superior a coward at the South Bridge in Concord, was killed by a British musket ball in Lexington nearly ten hours after the alarm rang in Sudbury Center. The second was Asahel Reed, a

member of Captain Nixon's Minute Man company. Both men are buried in the Old Burying Ground in Sudbury Center. Joshua Haynes, also a member of Nixon's minute company, was wounded. Lieutenant Elisha Wheeler's horse was shot out from under him during the fighting, and a musket ball passed through the folds of Thomas Plympton's coat, without injuring him, as he rode his horse.

The men of Sudbury continued to serve their country during the American War for Independence. At Bunker Hill, three Sudbury companies fought under the command of Colonel John Nixon, Major Nathaniel Cudworth, and Adjutant Abel Holden, Jr. When the British left Boston for good on March 17, 1776, the war had moved from New England into New York

Statue of Revolutionary War soldier in Sudbury Center Burying Ground. (Author)

and points south. Many Sudbury men, like others from New England towns, stayed behind to tend their farms and care for their families. John Nixon was promoted to brigadier general. Captains Abel Holden, Caleb Clapp, and Aaron Haynes continued their service. Over the course of the American Revolution, nearly five hundred men from a town of twenty-one hundred served. Sudbury produced one brigadier general, three colonels, two majors, two adjutants, two surgeons, twenty-four captains, and twenty-nine lieutenants. Twenty-six Sudbury men gave their lives for the patriot cause. Eight were wounded, including General John Nixon (then colonel) at Bunker Hill. Four men, during the course of the war, were taken prisoner and were never heard from again.

✯ REVOLUTIONARY WAR SITES TO VISIT TODAY IN SUDBURY ✯

The **Wayside Inn** (1716), one of America's oldest operating inns, is located on the Old Boston Post Road (Route 20) in Sudbury. Poet Henry Wadsworth Longfellow made the inn famous in his *Tales of a Wayside Inn* (1863), a collection of narrative poems that includes "Paul Revere's Ride." Henry Ford purchased the Wayside Inn and fifteen hundred acres of land in 1923 and refurbished the inn. Ford also moved the Red Stone schoolhouse to the site from nearby Sterling. (Myth has it that the ditty "Mary Had a Little Lamb" was based on the tale of one Mary Sawyer bringing her lamb to this very schoolhouse. However, the inn's historians today are dubious about this tale and say there is no solid evidence that Mary Sawyer was the Mary of the song.) Today the inn provides lodging and includes a restaurant, a colonial tavern, and a gift shop. A chapel, popular for weddings, and a gristmill also stand on the inn's spacious grounds.

Sudbury Center Burying Ground contains the statue of a Revolutionary War soldier. Standing among the weathered slate headstones is one that reads, "In memory of Deacon Josiah Haynes, who died in Freedom's Cause the 19th day of April, 1775 in the 79th year of his Age."

—Jay Cannon

✯ SOURCES ✯

Fischer, David H. *Paul Revere's Ride.* New York: Oxford, 1994.
French. *The Day of Lexington and Concord.* Boston: 1925.
Hudson, Alfred. *The History of Sudbury, Massachusetts, 1638–1889.* Sudbury: 1889.
Powers, John C. *We Shall Not Tamely Give it Up.* Boston: 1988.
Whitehill, Walter Muir. *In Freedom's Cause.* Boston: Lakeside Press, 1990.

Muster Roll of Massachusetts Towns
That Sent Men to the Concord Fight

★ ★ ★ ★ ★ ★ ★ ★ ★ ★ ★ ★ ★

Acton
Davis's Company
Hunt's Company
Robin's Company
Arlington
Locke's Company
Bedford
Moore's Company
Willson's Company
Beverly
Dodge's Company
Thorndike's Company
Shaw's Company
Billerica
Crosby's Company
Farmer's Company
Stickney's Company
Brookline
White's Company
Aspinwall's Company
Gardner's Company
Cambridge
Locke's Company
Thatcher's Company
Chelmsford
Barron's Company
Parker's Company
Concord
Barrett's Company
Brown's Company
Miles's Company
Minot's Company
Danvers
Epes's Company
Flint's Company
Hutchinson's Company
Lowe's Company
Page's Company
Prince's Company
Edmund Putnam's Company
John Putnam's Company

Dedham
Battle's Company
Bullard's Company
Draper's Company
Ellis's Company
Fairbanks's Company
Fuller's Company
Gould's Company
Guild's Company
Dracut
Coburn's Company
Russell's Company
Framingham
Edgell's Company
Emen's Company
Gleason's Company
Lexington
Parker's Company
Lincoln
Smith's Company
Stone's Company
Lynn
Bancroft's Company
Farrington's Company
Mansfield's Company
Newhall's Company
Parker's Company
Malden
Blaney's Company
Medford
Hall's Company
Needham
Aaron Smith's Company
Robert Smith's Company
Kingsbery's Company
Newton
Cook's or Marean's Company
Fuller's Company
Wiswall's Company

Reading
Bacheller's Company
Eaton's Company
Flint's Company
Walton's Company
Roxbury
Child's Company
Draper's Company
Whiting's Company
Stow
Whitcom's Company
Sudbury
Cudworth's Company
Haynes's Company
Locker's Company
Nixon's Company
Smith's Company
Stone's Company
Watertown
Bates's Company
Westford
Minot's Company
Parker's Company
Woburn
Belknap's Company
Fox's Company
Walker's Company

Source Coburn, Frank W. *Muster Roll of the Participating Companies of American Militia and Minute-Men in the Battle of April 19, 1775.* Eastern National, 1995.

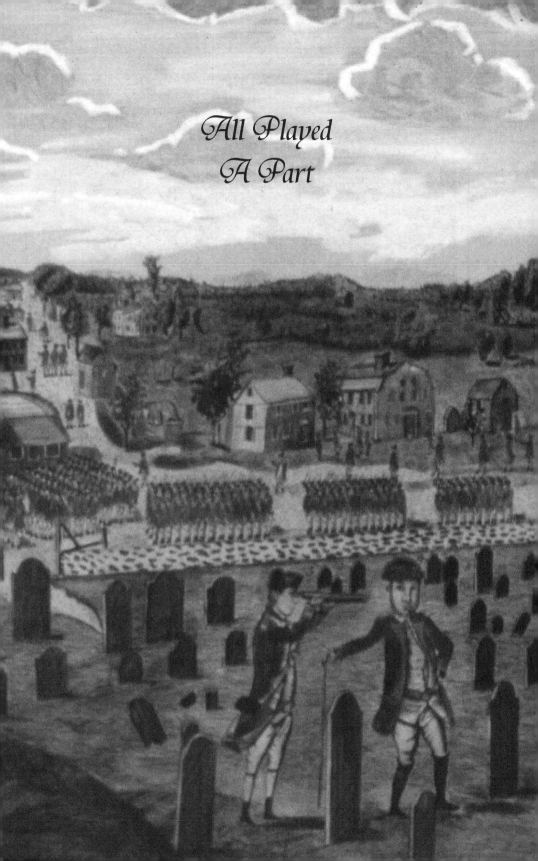

Mother Ruth Bathericke accepts the surrender of British soldiers at a reenactment in Arlington. (Menotomy Minute Men)

The Daughters
of Liberty

★ ★ ★ ★ ★ ★ ★ ★ ★ ★ ★ ★ ★ ★

Typically, in the telling of colonial American history, little mention is made of women and their roles in the Revolution's defining moments. Yet even surrounding the events of April 19, 1775, the daughters of America's liberty were visible and actively involved.

For example, might the actions of two ladies have significantly influenced events at Concord's North Bridge? Margaret Kemble Gage, the American-born wife of Boston's British military governor, Thomas Gage, was suspected of spying by both sides and harbored hopes that her husband's actions would not cause bloodshed. Some believe that she was the spy who leaked word of the Regulars' mission to Concord.

At age seventy-one, Concordian Martha Moulton was at home when the British soldiers entered town. When they burned captured matériel, the soldiers accidentally set fire to the Town House (flying sparks were to blame). Martha begged and harangued the British into extinguishing the blaze. But the resulting smoke, observed by the colonials mustered near Buttrick's farm, caused them to march to the town's rescue. Their approach precipitated the "shot heard 'round the world" and helped ignite the American Revolution.

Various women showed bravery that day, taking action to support the colonists' cause. Mrs. Amos Wood, Concord, saved military stores from British capture by insisting that a locked room harbored women, and thus the British left it unopened.

Hannah Barron (also spelled Barns or Burns) protected the provincial treasurer's chest, filled with money and important papers, by blocking soldiers' entrance to a tavern room, claiming the room and the trunk to be hers.

Abigail Wright, wife of the Concord tavern proprietor, is said to have secreted the church communion silver in soap barrels to prevent their being stolen. The same feat is also attributed to Mrs. Jeremiah Robinson, who supposedly gathered the same silver, hid it in her basement soap barrels, and barricaded her door against British intrusion.

Rebecca Barrett, wife of the colonel of Concord's militia, helped hide military stores and equipment about the farm, then remained at home to protect family and property from the expected British invasion. She fed the searching soldiers upon request, but refused money thrown at her, commenting that "we are commanded to feed our enemy" and that their coins were "the price of blood." Rebecca's actions saved valuable military matériel from discovery, her property from damage, and her son from arrest.

Another Barrett woman, Rebecca's granddaughter Melicent, age fifteen, had learned from a British officer how to roll powder cartridges. On the night of April 18, she supervised young women of Concord in preparing these items, which were most likely used against the Regulars at North Bridge.

For most wives and mothers, the approach of the British was a time of fear, trauma, uncertainty, and often sadness as their husbands and sons went off to fight. Lydia Mulliken of Lexington watched her fiancé, Dr. Samuel Prescott, ride off with Revere and Dawes to warn Concord of the British threat. During the Redcoats' retreat, they burned her house and shop.

From her house near Lexington Common, Ruth Harrington watched her husband Jonathan (standing with Parker's company) as he was struck by a British musket ball, then crawled to their house and died at her feet.

From the parsonage in Concord, Phoebe Bliss Emerson, the Concord minister's wife, would watch the North Bridge fight in dismay and wonder after the welfare of her husband, William.

Hannah Davis of Acton, like many wives, would see husband Isaac march to battle with intuition telling her he would not return alive. He died in the British volley at the bridge.

Other women contributed to freedom's stand too. Lincoln's Mary Flint Hartwell, hearing Dr. Prescott's night alarm for her Minute Man husband, handed their baby to a servant and ran a distance in the dark to warn Captain Smith of the approaching danger.

In Menotomy (Arlington), Mother Ruth Bathericke served the colonial cause with aplomb. While digging dandelions, she accepted the surrender of six fleeing British soldiers and later admonished them to "tell King George that an old woman took six of his grenadiers prisoner."

Throughout the day, many women gathered family valuables and their children, then fled to neighboring towns or into nearby woods for protection from the marauding British. Others, like Alice Stearns Abbott, remained at home (she lived in Watertown) and with her mother and sisters made cartridges and sent food to the patriots who fought. Later she would write, "I suppose it was a dreadful day in our house and sad indeed, for our brother, so dearly loved, never came home."

In Menotomy, Mrs. Butterfield would return home to find a bleeding, dying British officer in her bed. Though as a result she was accused of being a Tory, she cared for him some ten days until he died. When a neighbor threatened to kill the officer, Mrs. Butterfield protected him, shouting, "Only cowards would want to kill a dying man."

Some women went to extraordinary lengths in liberty's cause. At Pepperell, following the men's departure for Concord, the women met, formed a military company, dressed as men, armed themselves, and patrolled the town. Prudence Cummings, elected captain, captured a Tory officer at gunpoint. Such exploits would set the stage for female military heroes who served in the Revolutionary War, such as the following:

• Margaret Corbin, "Captain Molly," 1776, Battle of Fort Washington, New York, 1776, wounded and captured

• Mary Ludwig Hays, "Molly Pitcher," Battle of Monmouth, New Jersey, 1778

• Deborah Sampson, Continental Army soldier, 1782–1783, disguised as a man, wounded twice

Thus, from the earliest days, America's struggle for liberty and freedom was waged in part by its women, who showed ingenuity, valor, and steadfastness in supporting the cause. Such effort should never be overlooked, ignored, or taken lightly.

—D. Michael Ryan

★ Sources ★

Faran, Palmer. *Heroine of the Battle Road, Mary Hartwell.* Lincoln: Cottage Press, 1995.

Fischer, David H. *Paul Revere's Ride.* New York: Oxford, 1994.

French, Allen. *The Day of Concord and Lexington.* Boston: 1925.

Kehoe, Vincent J.-R. *We Were There!* Concord: unpublished manuscript, 1974.

Scudder, Townsend. *Concord: American Town.* 1947.

Shattuck, Lemuel. *History of Concord, Massachusetts.* Concord: 1835. Salem: reprinted by Higginson Book Co., 1995.

Children in the
American Revolution

★ ★ ★ ★ ★ ★ ★ ★ ★ ★ ★ ★ ★ ★ ★

With the onset of the American Revolution in 1775, many lives were changed drastically. Men cleaned their muskets and marched into battle. Women tended to their homes, sewing uniforms for the soldiers and watching over the property until the men returned. Yet during the war the lives of children were left mostly unaltered. "They heard stories of the war, but they were expected to do as they had always done." (Loeper) Most children lived on farms or in little villages and towns outside the city. Many avoided city dwelling because urban areas were considered dirty and unpleasant. At the time of the American Revolution, fewer than 3 million inhabitants lived in the thirteen colonies, compared to approximately one hundred times as many in the fifty states today.

Children seized many opportunities to participate in the Revolution, working for the colonies. In Concord, Cyrus, the son of Major Joseph Hosmer, was ten years old on April 19, 1775, when the British arrived. Mrs. Hosmer could not find Cyrus after the British had searched her house, looking for supplies. She overtook her son on the way to town. He was crying and claiming he knew his uncle Ben was dead and that he was going to see him at the Old North Bridge. His uncle actually was fine, but Cyrus was so upset by this experience that he put a lot of effort into aiding the colonists. As early as fifteen years of age, he delivered messages to places as far away as the river towns in Connecticut, telling people to hasten the arrival of their supplies. (Hosmer)

Another girl found a similar way to help. The oldest daughter of Colonel Ludington, sixteen-year-old Sybil, was wide awake one night when an exhausted messenger rode up to her house, warning the colonel that the British were going to attack Danbury, Connecticut (very close to her own home town of Mahopac), to seize its stores of ammunition, food, and so on. Since the rider was too tired to keep sending out the alarm, the colonel asked

Sybil to ride throughout the countryside and rouse his troops. As she galloped through the night, "she shouted the news and warned families to be ready to flee if the British should come that way." (Sybil Ludington) When she finally arrived back home at dawn, the colonel's regiment was already moving out towards Danbury. Thanks to her midnight ride, she soon came to be known as the "female Paul Revere."

Teenager Melicent Barrett discovered an unusual way to work for her cause. Her grandfather and father had set up a provisions business during the French and Indian War and continued it until around 1774. A young British officer often came to Melicent's house on the business of collecting these provisions and, while waiting, entertained himself by talking loyalty with Melicent, delighting in her rash rebel replies. Once he asked her, "What would they do if it became necessary for the Colonies to resist [the British rule] as there was not a person who even knew how to make cartridges?" (Swain) Melicent responded that the colonists would merely use their powder horns and bullets as if they were shooting bears. The officer felt this to be too "barbarous" and showed Melicent how to make a cartridge by whittling pine to the proper shape and cutting out the paper.

It is said that Melicent, with her new knowledge, soon had all the young ladies of Concord producing cartridges under her superintendence. The only male to help her was her younger brother, who drove the last load of cartridges from the house as the British came into sight on April 19, 1775. The scissors that Melicent reputedly used are preserved at the Concord Free Public Library.

Many boys in their teens actually found themselves in the middle of battles. Most drummers for the Minute Men were "young boys whose role gave them a sense of importance" in the fight for independence. (Ryan) William Diamond, a nineteen-year-old, was the drummer for the Lexington militia. He sounded the fateful call to arms on Lexington Green on April 19 when the colonial militia and the British fought for the first time. William's musical companion was Jonathan Harrington, a seventeen-year-old fifer. In Concord, the young fifer John Buttrick, only fifteen years old, played a tune while Samuel Derby beat out a rhythm on his drum to assemble troops there.

Isaac Muzzy, another young adolescent, stood, musket in hand, with the Lexington militia at dawn on April 19 as the Redcoats rounded the bend. Unfortunately, Isaac was badly wounded and died that day at his father's feet. One other boy, fourteen-year-old Edward Barber, ran to one of the windows in his house in Charlestown to watch the British march by. A Regular "leveled his musket and killed the boy with a single shot."

Some children took part in the Revolution through small, resistant boycotts. Eleven-year-old Anna Green Winslow vowed in her diary to wear only dresses and linens made from cloth manufactured in the colonies, not that imported from Britain. Many other children pledged not to drink tea, considered an incredibly fashionable beverage in those days because the only tea available was imported from Britain.

Children of the eighteenth century were treated very differently than they are today. Youths were looked upon as miniature adults who needed discipline to shape them into grown men and women. They dressed like their parents and were brought up to expect hard work during long days as part of their regular lives. Children did not have many of the opportunities available to those today. They were expected to be "seen and not heard, bawl not in speaking," and "walk not cheek by jole" but to "fall respectively behind and always give the wall to superiors." (Glubok)

Yet during the years of the Revolution, despite the strict rules set by adults, many patriotic children took it upon themselves to stand up for liberty. After the war, when the thirteen original colonies took a unifying name and emerged as a fresh nation, people of the newly formed United States of America began to look at children with a new respect as the promising next generation.

—Stephanie Bowen

✷ SOURCES ✷

Glubok, Shirley. *Home and Child Life in Colonial Days.* New York: MacMillan, 1969.

Hosmer, Josephine. "Memoir of Joseph Hosmer." From *The Centennial of the Social Circle,* vol. 1, pages 114–118. Boston: The Riverside Press, 1882.

Loeper, John J. *Going to School in 1776.* Boston: McClelland and Stewart, 1973.

Ryan, D. Michael. "Grand Music and the Concord Conflict." Accessed December 31, 2000. http://www.concordma.com/magazine/jan99/musik.html

Swain, James P. Letter to Charles Thompson, Concord, March 24, 1875.

"Sybil Ludington." Mahopac Library Online. Accessed December 29, 2000. http://www.mahopaclibrary.org/history/html/sybil ludington.html

Black Americans'
Battle for Freedom

★ ☆ ★ ☆ ★ ☆ ★ ☆ ★ ☆ ★ ☆ ★ ☆ ★ ☆ ★

The Provincial Congress at Concord in October 1774 reflected upon "the propriety, that while we are attempting to free ourselves from our present embarrassments and preserve ourselves from slavery, that we also take into consideration the state and circumstances of the negro slaves."

On the eve of the Revolution, which was fought in order to avoid "the horrors of British slavery" and "maintain the natural rights of men," some twelve Concord families owned slaves. This peculiar institution, part of town life since 1708, included at its height some twenty men, women, and children. Better treated than their counterparts in some colonies, Concord slaves could exercise certain rights, had to be educated in the ways of God and religion, often were included as parts of the family they served, and could obtain freeman status.

Historically, laws prohibited blacks from serving in militias, but such laws were often ignored during American colonial wars because of manpower shortages. With the master's consent, a male slave could enter the military, but was rarely allowed to do so because of his great value to the owner.

Whites commonly feared that armed slaves might revolt. In 1768 this feeling was reinforced when a British officer was arrested in Boston for inciting blacks "to fight against their masters." In 1774, some Boston slaves supposedly offered their military service to British General Thomas Gage in exchange for their freedom. And even as their Minute Men and militia companies marched in response to the alarm on April 19, 1775, the remaining citizens of Framingham armed themselves in fear of a black uprising.

Despite these ambivalent feelings about black slaves, one man of African descent was prominent in an event that roused patriotic sentiment and engraved itself on the colonists' collective memory. The first of the five colonials killed by British musket fire at the "Boston Massacre" on March 5, 1773,

Gilbert Stuart portrait of a black flutist, thought to be Revolutionary War soldier and fifer Barzillai Lew (1743–1822) of Boston. (Diplomatic Reception Rooms, U.S. Department of State)

was Crispus Attucks, a man of mixed African and Native American ancestry. The five who died became martyrs for the colonial cause.

During the fall and winter of 1774, blacks (including Concordians) most likely did not drill with town militias. But as spring approached, bringing with it the threat of armed conflict with England, volunteers were sought, and in some instances they included blacks. Though no official records list negroes as serving in Concord's companies by 1775, one roll call seems to indicate Philip

Barrett (slave of Colonel James Barrett) present at a militia muster. Since he was only age fourteen, it is more likely that he accompanied the colonel but did not directly serve. This may also have been the case with several other Concord slaves.

In addition to Barrett, others in Concord who owned slaves in 1775 included:

• Tory and former slave trader Duncan Ingraham, whose slave was named Cato

• John Cuming, a town meeting moderator, doctor, and colonel whose slave was named Brister

• Militia captain George Minot, whose slave was named Caesar

• Muster master Samuel Whitney, whose slave was named Casey

• Ralph Waldo Emerson's grandfather and Concord's minister, the Reverend William Emerson, whose slaves were named Frank, Phillis, and Cate

• Deacon Simon Hunt, whose slave was named Caesar

• Tory religious activist Dr. Joseph Lee, whose slave was named Cato

A few records document blacks from other towns who fought against British Regulars alongside their white townsmen on April 19, 1775. Prince Estabrook, a member of Parker's Lexington militia, fought and was wounded at the Lexington Common. At Concord's North Bridge, Caesar Jones (with Lieutenant Timothy Jones), Cambridge Moore, and Caesar Prescott were most likely in the Bedford ranks. The town of Bedford has erected a memorial to these black soldiers in the Town Burying Ground. Caesar Bason (later killed at Breed's Hill) may have represented Westford at North Bridge. Numerous towns counted black men in their ranks as they marched to pursue the fleeing British troops eastward along the Battle Road.

One Concord story of April 19 centers on Cato Ingraham, who stood at his owner's house, hands behind his back, as the Regulars approached. A British officer (possibly Major Pitcairn), believing Cato had a weapon, pointed a pistol to his head and demanded his arms. Unflustered, Cato raised his left, then his right arm, noting that those were the only arms he possessed.

Heroic tales of local people of color are recorded on April 19, including those of Menotomy's Cuff Cartwright, who ignored British bribes and rode to spread the alarm through town, and mulatto David Lamson, who led the "old men" of Metonomy in the capture of a British supply wagon.

Although maybe not involved at the North Bridge fight, Concord's blacks distinguished themselves in later military service. Philip Barrett marched in July 1775, enlisted in Captain Heald's company in 1779, served a six-month tour at West Point, and never returned to Concord. Brister (Cuming) Freeman served under Colonel John Buttrick at Saratoga in 1777, witnessed British general Burgoyne's surrender, enlisted again in 1779, and earned his freedom.

He later returned to Concord, where he settled and married. His burial site in Lincoln, next to five British soldiers, was noted by Thoreau in *Walden*. Caesar Minot served in the patriot army for three months in 1775–1776 and then signed for a three-year enlistment, returning to Concord at war's end. After a confrontation with his owner's son, Casey Whitney enlisted in the army, was later freed, and also returned to live in Concord.

Though some Concordians had opposed slavery and supported its abolition, a General Court resolve on the matter was vetoed in 1771 by Governor Hutchinson. By 1780, however, the Massachusetts State Constitution was ratified after a Bill of Rights was added, which included a ban on slavery.

The military role of slaves and freemen in the American Revolution should neither be ignored nor minimized. Their bearing of arms would help gain freedom for a nation and often for themselves while raising the hopes of a people.

John Jack was perhaps Concord's most famous slave because of the memorable epitaph on his tombstone. He is buried near the summit of the Old Hill Burying Ground near Monument Square in Concord Center. His epitaph, written in 1773 by Daniel Bliss, a Concord Tory, reads in part, "God wishes man free, man wills us slaves. I will as God wills; God's will be done."

Today the names of colonial black Concordians are memorialized in some of the town's place names. Jennie Dugan Road, Jennie Dugan Spring, Brister's Hill Road, and Peter Spring Road are all named for slaves who, after gaining their freedom, settled in these sections of Concord.

—D. Michael Ryan

★ SOURCES ★

Elliott, Barbara K., and Janet W. Jones. *Concord: Its Black History, 1636–1860.* Concord School Department, 1976.

McManus, Edgar J. *Black Bondage in the North.* 1973.

Piersen, William D. *Black Yankees.* 1988.

Sabin, Douglas. *The Role of Blacks in the Battle of April 19, 1775.* Minute Man National Historical Park, National Park Service, 1987 (Archives).

Trumbull, Joan. *Concord and the Negro.* Concord: 1944.

Native Americans
and the Revolution

★ ★ ★ ★ ★ ★ ★ ★ ★ ★ ★ ★ ★ ★

It has been suggested that the Revolutionary War cannot be understood properly without taking account of the participation of American Indians. Crispus Attucks, the first man to die in the Boston Massacre in 1770, was of mixed African and Native American ancestry. The name Attucks is Algonquian for "deer."

A Revolutionary War recruitment list from Plymouth, on the Massachusetts coast south of Boston, identifies certain enlistees from Plymouth county, a Wampanoag area, as Indian. (Gardner) Eighteen men from sixteen to thirty-four years of age were enlisted in five regiments, those of Lieutenant Colonel White, T. Cushing, Major Cary, Colonel C. O. Cotton, and Lieutenant Colonel Hall. Some of the enlistees' names are unmistakably Native American: Joshua Compsett, Parm Mouth, Benjamin Unket, Isaac Wickums, Samuel Word, and Caesar Meria, a sixteen-year-old drummer. They came from eight towns: Bridgewater, Kingston, Marshfield, Middleborough, Pembroke, Plymouth, Rochester, and Scituate.

The Wampanoag community of Mashpee on Cape Cod suffered particularly heavily in the Revolutionary War. One Barnstable regiment lost 25 out of 26 men, and the total loss for Mashpee was half the male population (more than 50). By 1788 there were only 25 men and 110 women of unmixed aboriginal descent remaining in Mashpee.

Before and during the war a different kind of struggle had also been taking place for control over Mashpee land. In 1760, Reuben Cognehew, a Mashpee leader, traveled to England to complain to the newly enthroned George III that white guardians placed over them by the Massachusetts legislature were forcing them to cede their land to white settlers, reducing the Mashpees to destitution. King George III prevailed on the legislature to give the Mashpees greater autonomy. But their short-lived freedom was lost after the Revolution, when the Mashpees became the equivalent of colonials for the newly liberated

"On the March": Sketch of a Mohegan on the road from Stockbridge to offer his help in the siege of Boston. (Kenneth Hamilton)

and independent dominant white Americans of European descent.

Like the Mashpees, the Hassana-misco Nipmuc in Grafton had been assigned white guardians who went off to fight in the Revolutionary War, but their replacements were incompetent, further reducing the circumstances of Nipmuc families. Forbears of the Cisco family, which has produced leaders in this century, had to sell most of their land at that time to survive. The Nipmuc, who were not getting along well with their white neighbors, tended to be Loyalists.

More affected were the descendants of Natick, a "praying town" west of Boston, one of the communities of Christian Indians founded by Minister John Eliot. Following the Revolution, Natick had lost all its males, leaving only widows and children.

Indian peoples viewed the American Revolution as an anticolonial war of liberation, but the threat to Native Americans' freedom often came from their colonial neighbors rather than from London, and Indians' colonial experience did not end with American independence. (Calloway)

Despite the loss of men, women, land, and possessions in the centuries following European arrival and long after the American Revolution, the Algonquian peoples of Massachusetts have shown adaptability and persistence, and in this century have felt able once again to claim their identity openly. Today on any summer weekend a visitor may find a pow-wow (dance celebration) in progress in some Massachusetts town and is welcome to participate in the revival of American Indian culture and society that is taking place across America.

The following names show the influence of Algonquian words in place names in and around Concord:

Massachusetts. Our state is named for the Massachusett tribe of coastal Algonquians. The state seal has always included an American Indian, a design that has been protested frequently by Native Americans.

Musketaquid, meaning "grassy, reedy river." This is the Algonquian name for today's Concord.

Menotomy, meaning "swift running waters." This is the name that Algonquians and, later, early English settlers gave to the village between Cambridge and Lexington—today's Arlington.

Annursnac, meaning "the summit or lookout." This one of Concord's three large hills retains its original Algonquian name.

Nashawtuc, meaning "between two rivers." Nashawtuc Hill in Concord is between the Assabet and Sudbury Rivers before they converge to form the Concord River.

Punkatasset, meaning "shallow brook hill." It was at Punkatasset Hill that Concord's militia and Minute Men gathered after their strategic withdrawal from Concord village as more than seven hundred British Regulars marched into Concord from Lexington early on the morning of April 19, 1775.

Assabet, meaning "a swampy place." The Assabet River starts in the town of Westborough and winds for thirty-two miles through primal woodlands as well as past mill cities before joining the Sudbury River to form the Concord River. Egg Rock, where the two rivers merge, was a gathering spot for Native Americans for thousands of years. All three rivers are popular with canoeists and kayakers today.

Squaw, meaning "woman"; sachem, meaning "chief." Squaw Sachem Trail in Concord is named for the woman who, in 1637, as leader of a local band of Algonquian Native Americans, negotiated the sale of "six myles square" of their land at Musketaquid to British settlers—land which had been renamed Concord.

—Shirley Blancke

✹ SOURCES ✹

Blancke, Shirley, and Barbara Robinson. *From Musketaquid to Concord: The Native and European Experience.* Concord: Concord Museum, 1985.

Calloway, Colin G. *The American Revolution in Indian Country.* Cambridge: Cambridge University Press, 1995.

Campisi, Jack. *The Mashpee Indians: Tribe on Trial.* Syracuse: Syracuse University Press, 1991.

Gardner, Russell (Great Moose). Personal communication from Gardner, the late Wampanoag tribal historian, about a document discovered by Jeremy Bangs, formerly visiting curator of Pilgrim Hall in Plymouth.

Huden, John C. *Indian Place Names in New England.* New York: Heye Foundation, 1962.

Mandell, Daniel R. *Behind the Frontier: Indians in Eighteenth-Century Eastern Massachusetts.* University of Nebraska Press, 1996.

Peters, Russell. *The Wampanoags of Mashpee.* Nimrod Press, 1987.

Jewish Contributions to
the Fight for Liberty

★ ★ ★ ★ ★ ★ ★ ★ ★ ★ ★ ★ ★ ★ ★

T here was much recent controversy about naming the new bridge that spans the Charles River between Boston and Charlestown—the Leonard P. Zakim Bunker Hill Bridge. A noted human rights activist, Zakim was director of the Antidefamation League of B'nai B'rith. Reports of anti-Semitism surfaced from a small group of Charlestown residents, one of whom was quoted in the *Boston Globe* as saying, "I don't see the relationship between a bridge in this area and a Jewish fellow . . . there were no Jews at Bunker Hill." (Lewis) A brief review of the role of the Jews in the Revolutionary era should add some needed historical perspective. It is a tale seldom told.

The first group of Jews to settle in North America were twenty-three refugees from Recife, Brazil, in 1654. They were escaping persecution that resulted when Portugal seized control of Brazil from Holland. They settled in New Amsterdam (present-day New York). They were descendants of Sephardic (Spanish and Portuguese) Jews who had been expelled from Spain in 1492 and from Portugal in 1497. Like their forbears, who had been denied basic human rights for over sixteen hundred years in their wanderings among the restrictive ghettos of Europe, the Jews who landed in the small Dutch town of New Amsterdam had little freedom. They were forbidden by law to own land, own a house, worship in public, hold public office, vote, travel, serve in the military, and enter most trades and professions.

After the British recaptured New York ten years later, many of these restrictions stayed in place in various colonies. Especially onerous to religious Jews were laws prohibiting voting and office holding unless they swore oaths "as Christians." In Puritan Massachusetts in the seventeenth and eighteenth centuries, these restrictions were more severe than in most other colonies. Puritans fled England so that they could practice religion without interference from others; however, once in New England, they did not tolerate followers of other religions. They viewed Jews mainly as targets for conversion. The first professor of Hebrew at Harvard College was an Italian Jew named Judah Moniz, who in

1722 was persuaded to convert to Christianity as a necessary qualification to teach there.

Because of these objectionable religious restrictions, all but a handful of early Jewish American settlers avoided Boston. They clustered instead in six cities along the Eastern seaboard: Newport, New York, Philadelphia, Charleston, Richmond, and Savannah.

These cities had the framework for Jewish communities: observant families, synagogues, rabbis, benevolent societies, and the means to earn livings. But there were still precious few Jews in America. At the time of the Revolution it is estimated that only twenty-five hundred of the 2.5 million Americans (or 0.1 percent) were Jewish. (Marcus)

Haym Salomon was a Polish immigrant who settled in New York in about 1772. There he joined the patriotic cause and became active in the Sons of Liberty. He was captured by the British, accused of spying for the patriots, and sentenced to hang. He escaped and fled with his young family to Philadelphia. There he prospered as an import-export broker.

Salomon volunteered his services to raise money for the insolvent Continental Congress, which was often so broke that it could not pay American soldiers. Relying only on his honest reputation and his good word, he was able to raise money by selling bills of exchange from France and Spain, so the troops could be paid and desertions avoided. When he died, Haym Salomon was destitute, having exhausted his private resources for his new country. (Russell, Wolf)

Benjamin Nones came to Philadelphia from Bordeaux, France, in time to fight for the patriots. He was captured by the British in the siege of Charleston and not released until the Battle of Yorktown. He later became a major in the Pennsylvania militia. In 1800 he was involved in a political feud and was subjected to a personal anti-Semitic attack in a Philadelphia paper. He replied with a ringing attack against anti-Semitism: "But I am a Jew. I am so—and so were Abraham and Isaac and Moses and the prophets, and so too were Christ and his apostles. I feel no disgrace in ranking with such society may be subject to the illiberal buffoonery of such men as your correspondents." (Rezneck)

Hundreds of other Jewish soldiers and sailors fought in the Revolution and supported it. They included Phillip Russell, a surgeon's mate at Valley Forge; Colonel David Franks, an aide to George Washington; a "Jew Company," which fought in South Carolina; Moses Myers, who fought in Virginia; and the Sheftall family, who fought and were captured in Savannah. In Manhattan's Chatham Square Cemetery lie twenty-two Jewish soldiers who fought in the Revolutionary War. Many had sacrificed their lives for their new country, just like the patriots who were killed during the three British assaults at Bunker Hill in 1775. New evidence has surfaced that a Jewish soldier, Abraham Solomon, participated in the Battle of Bunker Hill. (Rezneck)

In 1790, seven years after the Revolution was over, President George Washington delivered a speech to the synagogue in Newport, Rhode Island. He stated that "happily the Government of the United States . . . gives to bigotry no sanction, to persecution no assistance." After two thousand years of wandering, Jews—and all other Americans—were at last guaranteed religious freedom.

Here is an important footnote to the question "What have Jews got to do with Bunker Hill ?" In 1825, on the fiftieth anniversary of the Battle of Bunker Hill, a cornerstone was laid for a proposed monument. But because funding dwindled, the monument was unfinished fourteen years later. Boston industrialist Amos Lawrence offered ten thousand dollars if the remaining funds could be raised. No backers appeared until a Jewish philanthropist from New Orleans, Judah Touro, a man born one day before the Battle of Bunker Hill, broke the impasse by contributing ten thousand dollars. The inscription at the base of the monument recognizes both the differences and shared humanity and aims of Lawrence and Touro: "Christian and Jew, they carry out one plan, / For though of different faith, each is in heart a man." (Sarna)

Hopefully, the Leonard P. Zakim Bunker Hill Bridge will honor *both* the men who gave their lives at Bunker Hill in 1775 and Lenny Zakim, who spent his life building bridges between the communities of Boston.

☆ SOURCES ☆

Andrews, Joseph L, Jr., M.D. "To Bigotry No Sanction: The Role of Jews in the American Revolution." *Sons of the American Revolution Magazine,* Louisville, winter 2001.

Faber, Eli. *A Time for Planting: The First Migration, 1654–1820.* Baltimore: Johns Hopkins University Press, 1992.

Knight, Vick. "Send for Haym Salomon!" Alhambra: Borden, 1976.

Lewis, R. "A Gap Left Unbridged." *Boston Globe,* January 6, 2001.

Marcus, Jacob. *The Colonial American Jew, 1492–1776.* Detroit: Wayne State, 1970.

Pool, David. *Portraits Etched in Stone: Early Jewish Settlers, 1682–1831.* New York: Columbia University, 1952.

———. *An Old Faith in a New World: Portrait of Shearith Israel, 1654–1954.* New York: Columbia University, 1955.

Rezneck, Samuel. *Unrecognized Patriots: The Jews in the American Revolution.* Westport, Connecticut: Greenwood, 1975.

Russell, C. *Haym Salomon and the Revolution.* New York: Cosmopolitan, 1930.

Sarna, J. and E. Smith, editors. *The Jews of Boston.* Boston: Combined Jewish Philanthropies of Greater Boston, 1995.

Wolf, Edwin and M. Whiteman. *The History of the Jews of Philadelphia, From Colonial Times to the Age of Jackson.* Jewish Publication Society, 1956.

Index